The Making of Vince Carter

A BASKETBALL MOM'S MEMOIR

MICHELLE VERNAE CARTER

Copyright © 2023 Michelle Vernae Carter

The Making of Vince Carter: A Basketball Mom's Memoir

All rights reserved. The use of any part of this publication, reproduced, transmitted in any form or by any means, electronic, mechanical, photocopying, recording or otherwise without the prior written consent of Michelle Vernae Carter is an infringement of the copyright law.

Printed by Book Baby Publishing in 2023

For information, address Paris Media Group Subsidiary Rights Department via publishing@parismedia.org. For information about special discounts for bulk purchases, please contact Paris Media Group via info@parismedia.org. The Paris Media Group speakers' bureau can bring authors to your live event. For more information or to book an event, contact Paris Media Group via info@parismedia.org.

Cover art: Don Traub based on photos provided by Michelle Vernae Carter
Editorial and design work: purebold.co.uk
All photos are from the Carter family collection.

ISBN 979-8-218-15907-8 (hardcover)

ISBN 979-8-218-15908-5 (paperback)

Contents

Foreword i
Acknowledgements iii
1. What I Knew: The Making of an NBA All-Star 1
2. Late to the Game 11
3. Dunking in the Sixth Grade 21
4. Volleyball, Football, Basketball... Band? 31
5. The Quest for the State Championship 51
6. College Recruitment Chaos 65
7. The Carolina Way 77
8. Should He Stay or Should He Go? The NBA Draft 91
9. From Rookie to Vinsanity 105
10. For the Record—What Happened in Toronto 119
11. Going for Olympic Gold 139
12. From Canada to the Peach State
    (and Places in Between) 149
13. Vices Everywhere (and You Love Some of Them) 169
14. Here's What I Know 179
15. What's Next 189
Afterword 193
Vince Carter's Career Data and Statistics 195
Vince Carter's Awards and Honors 199
About the Author 201
Sources 205

The Making of Vince Carter

Foreword

I would guess that the person who knows me—Vincent "Vince" Lamar Carter—better than anyone else is my mom, Michelle Vernae Carter. After all, I have been with her, and she has been with me, all of my life. She has cared for me when I could not care for myself. She has made plans for my life when I didn't know how to plan. She has guided and advised me to lessen the chances of stumbling through life. I suppose she had in her mind a time when she would be comfortable letting me fly solo. Yet, I know that she will *never* let me soar completely alone. For me it is comforting to know that my safety net will be there as long as she lives.

There is no one more capable of telling my story, not even me. For my parents put me on the path to enjoy my childhood and grow into a responsible adult. Now that I look back, I am thankful that I was smart enough to listen and follow their lead.

Vince Carter

The Making of Vince Carter

Acknowledgements

Vince Carter: I thank you for always trying to do things the right way. You are a parent's dream, although you can be stubborn at times. You most often figure it out. The memories you have provided for me, your mom, will always be cherished.

Jason Glenn, my dear friend: you have changed my life in ways that I could not imagine. Your gentle push and encouragement were what I needed. Thus, my vow to tell my story has come to fruition. You will always hold a special place in my heart.

Peggy Green, my late mom: she always wanted my two sisters and me to be the best we could be, and to do our best. Actually, she demanded it. There were times when I certainly didn't like the strong hand of "mama". Today, I wish that she was here so I could thank her over and over again.

Ann Smith, my longtime assistant and friend; also Vince's seventh grade Language Arts Teacher (partially responsible for all of that subject–verb agreement): you've always been there for me, and that is priceless.

Claudine "Claude" Riban: thank you for your assistance in helping me to navigate through chapters and assist with the research for this book. I appreciate your views as a "fan" of Vince Carter and the NBA.

Thank you to anyone who has ever uttered a prayer for me or has wished me well.

The Making of Vince Carter

1

What I Knew: The Making of an NBA All-Star

When parents of superstar athletes talk (or brag) about their kids, they usually say they just knew their kid was going to be great some day. From age 6 or 7 or 10 they knew that their amazing little athlete was going to go pro—and one day star in the Superbowl, or World Series, or Olympics.

They talk like going pro was predetermined for their child from the day they were born, and their child's eventual success was a given. In their stories, they often elevate their child's destiny straight to the pros too; college is a mere truck stop on the super-highway to their kid's pro career glory.

Well, my son Vincent could dunk the basketball by grade six, and I was still not one of those parents. Never was. I confess right here and now: I didn't believe that my son, Vince Carter, was good enough to go pro until 1996, two years before the 1998 National Basketball Association (NBA) draft, where he was selected #5.

That's right, I didn't know. I didn't know when his high school basketball team was runner up in the Florida State Championship. I didn't know when his team won that same title the next year. I didn't know when he was named "Florida's Mr. Basketball"—the honor given to the best player in the state each year.

I didn't know for sure he'd go pro after Vincent was approached by 77 different National Collegiate Athletic Association (NCAA) basketball programs to play for their school. I didn't even know after Vince was named a prestigious McDonald's All-American, then played in their All-American East vs. West game on national TV. He won the McDonald's Slam Dunk Contest too, also on national TV.

I didn't even know for sure Vince would become a pro after the first time he went to the NCAA Final Four with the UNC Tar Heels. I wasn't fully certain the second time either, when his team returned to the Final Four the next year. That was one sweet squad.

Parents of great athletes tell some great stories about their kids, to be sure, and invariably they recognized their child's talent as something special when it emerged. But most of these parents have chosen to see everything from an optimist's perspective, in terms of the best-case scenario. I don't think this is wise.

I'm here to tell you that taking the optimistic perspective about your child's athletic potential, and this perspective only, is a fool's game. I was never one of these overly optimistic sports parents, and this book is in part about why this wasn't me. I like to think readers may benefit from knowing my past, my skeptical approach, and my now retrospective wisdom.

Whether or not you yourself are a parent of a gifted athlete, perhaps a future pro athlete, there is much to be gained from holding a more pessimistic approach to your athlete's future.

My motto is "Plan B mode until Plan A actually happens."

Let me start by explaining what I knew back then. "What I knew back then," means the knowledge I picked up during my own upbringing that affected the way I chose to raise my own children when I was still a very young parent myself. During some of Vince's childhood, I was a single parent to boot. Life came at me so fast; I didn't always understand the forces that shaped my early decisions as a parent, but now, when I look back, it's more in focus.

One thing that has remained in vivid focus my whole life is just how many gifted athletes lived in the Miami, Florida, area when I grew up there. At the youth sports level—including Little League, Pop Warner Football, and our local varsity high school teams—there was so much incredible athletic talent everywhere. This was true for grown men too, many of whom worked in construction, building up greater Miami during the week, then showing off their prime baseball or basketball skills in amateur league play or pick-up games on the weekend. I used to marvel at what some of these amateur athletes could do. It sure seemed like a lot of them should be playing pro ball somewhere.

There was this one teenage boy I knew, who—I swear—could throw a football an entire city block. He'd set up his friend at one corner at a busy intersection, then run all the way down the street until he stood at the next intersection. He'd step back and release that ball so perfectly and with so much spin, it'd fly up, follow a high arc, and just sail into the ready arms of his receiver-friend standing on the sidewalk one city block away. Sometimes he'd show off for the local girls like me and my sisters, and the ball would go sailing over his friend's head and straight into traffic.

For reference, the entire length of an American football field, including the length of both endzones, is 120 yards, or 360 feet. The typical block lengths in Miami are 400 feet. That means this teenager could easily throw the ball over 40 feet more than the length of a football field. I remember bragging about him to my "bonus dad"—my mom's second husband (we never used the term "step" to describe family members).

I told my bonus dad that I was certain this boy who could throw a block was going pro someday, that he was going to be as famous in football as Willie Mays was in baseball. At that time, in the mid-1960s, there were no prominent African American quarterbacks in the National Football League (NFL) to root for yet.

I was born when segregation was still a sorry reality in most of the USA, thus I grew up in an African American enclave. My hometown was Liberty City, which is now a northwest neighborhood of Miami. Nowadays, in South Florida, everything is paved and developed, and it's difficult to tell where neighborhoods or towns begin or end.

During my childhood, however, there was some actual green space between communities. There were acres of palm groves, citrus orchards, dirt roads and open fields that separated communities, and Liberty City was its own little town, tucked safely away from the noise and bustle of downtown Miami. Liberty City eventually became one of Miami's more notorious neighborhoods, but while I grew up there it was thriving and safe.

I am blessed to have had the perfect mother for me. Tenacious in her protection, dogged about ensuring that I give my best, faithful to the core, humble, humorous, and wise. I am thankful to have my mother's love abiding with me. Whatever good emanating from me is inspired by the deposits made in me by my ancestors—my great grandmothers Blonzette Gabriel and Jane Herout, my grandmothers Annie Bell Westbrook and Emily Ross, my mom Peggy Green, my grandfather Clinton Gabriel and my dads Willie Harris and Clinton Green. My love of God and family, and my acceptance of all people, are trademarks of having been nurtured by this family of mine. I know from where my blessings and my hope come. My family made sure that this was understood.

But to return to Liberty City, it's a sad fact that by the

time I left town for college, it had begun its heartbreaking transition from the sleepy African American working- and middle-class community that I knew and loved, into something a little rougher and less amenable. This shift happened in part because lower income people of color, who were displaced by the building of the interstate "I-95," were migrating into the community, into hastily built, substandard low-income housing. But that's a whole other story, and not really mine to tell. I moved away from Liberty City as a teenager to go to college at Bethune-Cookman College (now Bethune-Cookman University) in Central Florida, and I never lived in South Florida again; I only returned to visit my family.

But back in the 1960s and early 1970s, when I lived there, Liberty City was a proud, independent community with decent schools, roads, churches and many single family homes, like the one my own family lived in. African American professionals and laborers would often work in downtown Miami, but lived in segregated communities.

Some professionals, however, like my uncle, lived in Miami proper, so segregation was beginning to break down. My uncle was a career police officer who eventually became Miami's top cop in 1985—Police Chief Clarence Dickson.

Uncle Clarence was both the first African American to become Miami's Police Chief and the first to graduate from the Miami Police Academy in 1960.

My mother, Peggy Green, was also a professional. She went back to college after having me, and studied at FAMU (Florida A&M University), and Nova University of Advanced Technology (now Nova Southeastern University). She eventually received her degree in Education and became an elementary school educator. She loved her teaching career, and in particular loved mentoring young teachers and spoiling her own students—if they behaved and took their lessons seriously.

My mother divorced my biological father when I was very

young and later remarried; her second husband, Clinton Green, was the man my two sisters and I lovingly nicknamed our "bonus dad." He was such a good-natured, kind, and loving man.

I was the eldest child; my younger sisters were Errolyn and Jennifer. We only saw my biological father sporadically while growing up. He lived in South Florida too, working as a long-distance truck driver.

My bonus dad strove to be a proper family man. He was determined to improve his own professional situation and our family's prospects. When I was a little girl, he had jobs as a liquor distributor for McKesson and Robbins (now McKesson Corporation). He was a very popular man-about-town who could conduct a friendly conversation with anyone.

My bonus dad wanted to do better in life professionally, so he did. He went back to school and received his Associate Degree. He worked diligently at his studies, began working as a banker, and was greatly respected in our community.

Eventually, he became Vice-President at the prestigious Bank of America. He showed our family the rewards that a combination of education, ambition, and hard work could bring. I was so proud of him, and I paid attention to his success.

My mom also strongly believed in the power of education; she was a school teacher after all. But, unlike my bonus dad who led by example, my mom used discipline as her primary motivational method. Let me tell you—she was strict as all get out.

I had two basic choices. Option 1 was "do well in school, make honor roll, and have some privileges like being allowed to hang out with friends, and do fun stuff like go to the movies with my friends." Option 2 was "don't do well in school, then your life becomes a prison in your room, trapped only with school books." Those were the only choices, and I never even got close to trying Option 2 because my mom could be that scary! I felt like Mom was a lot less scary to her students, whom she was stern with; but she also showered them, my sisters, and me with kindness when we followed the rules.

I had friends whose moms encouraged their daughters to be more social, get involved with sports, go to parties, and maybe even go to the dance with a nice boy; not my mom! In addition to being strict, I don't remember her laughing and goofing off with us kids all that much. She had fun and enjoyed herself when she and my bonus dad hosted weekend parties with their many friends. But getting a quality education was at the top in her list of priorities for her children. Being active in our local church—the Church of the Incarnation—was somewhere near the top also, but, even though we were active and devout, education always came first.

Because I was the eldest, I was obviously the object of my mom's first attempt at parenting—I was her test case, as it were. So I got to experience both what she got right and, to a higher degree than my sisters did, what she got wrong. Mom tended to be stricter with me, which I would come to appreciate later in life, because I developed a certain toughness as a result. This toughness in turn helped me better guide Vincent's education and youth sports career. But back then as a kid in Liberty City, dealing with my mom's disciplinarian ways was tough.

If you had told me as a teenager that I'd someday parent my own kids in ways a little reminiscent of my mom, I think I'd find that a wee bit troubling. But as I reflect on my early life, I'm starting to understand better where she was coming from.

To my mom, if you were a nice family, your kids did well in school, went to church, then went to college. Then they got a good job. That was the plan. That's what she did. She appreciated that school provided her with that path. I don't think it ever occurred to her—or my bonus dad—that excelling in sports was another pathway to a better life. They either didn't know how athletics, sports scholarships, and the pros really worked, or they were not interested. I'm not sure which it was.

Also keep in mind that I grew up during the final years of segregation in the USA, and there simply were not as many athletic scholarships available to African Americans. I remember applying to Bethune-Cookman College in Daytona Beach, one of the HBCU (Historically Black Colleges and Universities), because this was one of the few Florida schools that I knew for sure would accept me.

I was never encouraged to participate in youth or team sports by my own parents. If you know how obsessed Vince was with sports as a kid, you might find this shocking.

I did play a little intramural volleyball in high school, but that was my entire sports career. Sometimes, as a teen, I may have resented the role of being the "nice girl," who always made the honor roll, and I was rarely allowed to go to parties or dances. Now, however, I appreciate that the idea that "education matters most" was instilled in me at a young age. With my bonus dad's achievements, I also witnessed the rewards of education.

Back then, I could see that the nice well-behaved kids, who got good grades and college opportunities, usually came from families who emphasized doing well in school, no matter how much money their parents earned. Sometimes our local gifted young athletes came from families who cared about school, but just as often, they came from families who didn't put a premium on learning. They just hoped for the best. They had no plan.

Sadly, that boy who could throw the ball a city block came from a family where doing well in school wasn't important. I believe he dropped out of high school around age 16, which means he never ever got a chance to be recruited by a local college football program, much less get a shot at his dream of playing in the NFL. As he hadn't achieved decent grades—or in fact any grades—no college coaches ever came to scout him, there were no newspaper articles written about his amazing arm-strength, and he never even showed up in any team pictures in my senior yearbook. How sad.

I saw other talented young athletes from my town dream of the pros too, without the slightest understanding of how to get there. They didn't seem to know that the things they did in the classroom today translated into opportunities on the playing field or in the gym tomorrow.

At some level, Liberty City was paved, in part, with the broken dreams of some truly gifted athletes who never even got a shot because no one in their family circle emphasized education. I witnessed young men focused on the fundamentals of a game, instead of learning the fundamentals of life.

Even before college, I recall being skeptical about the chances of anyone in my home circle, even my own son Vince, becoming a professional athlete. I was certainly never taught that athletic talent was a realistic pathway to success. It seemed more like a mirage, or even a potential trap if the athlete failed to develop other useful life skills in case the pro career didn't work out.

To be fair, back then I still didn't fully understand how youth sports worked. I never had any exposure to elite youth sports, including basketball. This would soon change.

The Making of Vince Carter

2

Late to the Game

So, you may be wondering: if *I* was never encouraged to play youth sports, and if my family near-exclusively watched pro football as our shared TV sport, how did Vince Carter the Basketball Phenomenon ever happen?

Being a truly elite athlete is always some mix of genetics, environment and opportunity. That's really the base formula no matter where you live and play sports. I don't believe I had much pro-athlete DNA, and I was not raised in a sports-obsessed environment where participating in athletics was the norm. But, thanks to my family's focus on education, I did have opportunities. Eventually, I made my own opportunities, but first there was college.

Although I knew from a very early age that I would attend college some day, I did not have much say in which college it was. It was mostly my mom's decision, with minimal input from me and my bonus dad. I figured I would probably attend Nova University because that's where my mom went to college, and it was near home. My mom, however, had a different plan.

My mom was a controlling person, as you can probably tell by now, so you'd think she'd have picked a college for me that was closer to home—that she'd want to micromanage my college experience, like she had done with high school. That's what I expected to happen. So, I was genuinely surprised when she selected an out-of-area college for me: Bethune-Cookman College in Daytona Beach, Florida. By "out of area" I literally mean outside our local "305" telephone area code region which serves greater Miami. When you're 17 and have never left home to live on your own, any place that requires a long-distance phone call to reach home is far away and exotic. Even if it's just a four-hour car drive away from your house in Liberty City, as Bethune-Cookman College was.

There were, I think, three main reasons my mom selected Bethune-Cookman for me. One was because my family, my elders, greatly admired its founder and namesake, the famed civil rights activist and educator, Dr. Mary McLeod Bethune. Dr. Bethune was such a force for good in American education; I wouldn't even know where to begin listing her achievements and attributes. I strongly recommend reading one of the many books, or watching a documentary, about her amazing life if you want to learn more about great leadership.

Suffice it to say that symbolically, to my mom, Dr. Bethune was like a Greek goddess on the Mount Olympus of Learning.

I was so inspired by Dr. Bethune that in 2022, decades after graduating from college, I became a key member of a team of people who were able to posthumously honor and recognize Dr. Mary McLeod Bethune by having a marble statue of her placed in our nation's National Statuary Hall, located in the Capitol Building in Washington, DC. This Statuary Hall is full of statues of famous Americans, and most of the honorees were voted into the Hall by individual American States.

The addition of Dr. Bethune's statue to the Statuary Hall is something I am very proud of, and I believe my mom, now in heaven, is also proud of. The statue of Dr. Bethune is, in fact, the first statue of an African American voted into the Statuary Hall by state legislators.

Mom's second reason for choosing Bethune-Cookman was the college's long-standing affiliation with the Christian religion, specifically the United Methodist Church. Although I was raised in the Episcopalian tradition, United Methodists were like our first cousins in what is known as mainline Protestantism. Methodists were also famed for their seriousness, their rigor, and the great institutions of higher learning they founded like Duke and Emory Universities. That all must have appealed to Mom.

The third reason was the most practical. Bethune-Cookman was created to educate and nurture teachers. In fact, when Bethune-Cookman College became a fully accredited four-year college in 1941, every member of its very first graduating class received a Bachelor of Science degree in Elementary Education. They were all elementary schoolteachers like my mom.

That was Mom's life plan for me, to have me become a schoolteacher just like her. But I did not pursue a degree in elementary education; I adapted her plan. At first, I thought about getting a degree in economics; I really liked my economics classes and made straight As in them. But I made friends at Bethune-Cookman with some girls who thought studying economics was strictly for nerds and that I should get my degree in business instead. I knew I liked business: I liked how my bonus dad made deals and always seemed to be getting a better job in the business world. Eventually, he got so good with money that he became a banking executive as mentioned already. I knew businesspeople usually earned more than teachers, too. But a part of me wanted to please my mom. Even as a college student, I wanted to please her.

I learned Bethune-Cookman offered a degree in Business Education, and, just like that, my problem was solved. With a Business Education degree, I could be a businessperson or a teacher. Mom approved of my new plan, given that I would always have a teaching degree to fall back on if the business world didn't work out. We both liked having options. As my mom said, "there always will be children to teach."

To this day I'm glad my mom chose Bethune-Cookman College. In addition to my work honoring Dr. Bethune, I also still choose to live in Volusia County, Florida, where the now Bethune-Cookman University is located. But back then at age 17 I didn't really plan on living away from home, and I vividly recall how strange and lonely it was to suddenly be on my own in my college dorm room as a teenager. This is a feeling I never forgot, and something I worried about when it was time for Vince to leave home for college.

I wasn't that deeply involved in Liberty City life beyond family, a few close friends, and church. Vince, however, was easily the most popular kid in his high school, and yet also a homebody somehow. He was much more connected to his native community. I genuinely worried about him being suddenly uprooted for college. More on that later.

So, did I play any sports in college? Absolutely not. I did, however, love going to the football games to cheer the Wildcats. At halftime I loved watching the routines of the famed female Bethune-Cookman dance line—the 14 Karat Gold Dancers. This popular dance group is usually just called "14K," and they were a big deal at my college back in the early 1970s, and still are today.

Look them up on YouTube; 14K has performed many times on national TV, at football game half times, and at elite dance competitions. If you think they are risqué now, I swear they were already like that back when I was there, with their tiny form-fitting outfits, spandex and sequins. Society was more modest back then too, so their scanty outfits and seductive moves were much more scandalous. How a college so strongly associated with the United Methodist Church historically developed this dance line is truly one of the great mysteries of life! But hey, I was still a teenager back then and thought they were so cool. Somehow, in my mind, I also thought I had a chance of making their squad, even though I had never studied dance or participated in my high school bands. I did, however, love to dance. Still do. So, I watched their routines carefully, I took mental notes, and I practiced their sexy moves when I thought no one was watching. But then I made a near-fatal error.

My parents would regularly visit me at college, especially during football weekends, when our team, the Bethune-Cookman Wildcats, played at home. I would, of course, sit in the stands and root for the team with my mom, dad, and other visiting family members like my sisters. My sister Errolyn was even a cheerleader for Bethune-Cookman.

Well, one football weekend, full of youthful dumbness, I told my mom I planned to try out for the 14K dancers. You'd think I'd told my mom I'd gotten knocked-up by the Devil himself for how she reacted, and how her eyes went wide. She looked at me, simultaneously calm and furious, and said, "if you do that, and you make the squad, when you're out there during halftime performing, I will come out on the field and snatch you off of that field." Prudently, I decided to put my dance career on hold for ever.

To this day I will never forget the fury of that moment. But I also knew there was something wrong about how she handled it. I could appreciate that the 14K squad back then was too risqué for her tastes, and completely opposite to her vision of the respectable life she wanted for me. But I also knew it was wrong that she always did this to me. She had this tendency to crush my interest in anything fun, even when my interests were innocent, which they all were. While Mom made sure I was on the right track in life, and I thank her dearly for this, I also believe I may have talents I never got a chance to discover.

Sometime after my dance ambitions were annihilated, I believe I made some kind of unspoken promise to myself to never restrict my future children's opportunities and interests—especially in such a harsh and automatic way. I was pursuing my degree in business education too, and in my coursework I was also learning about child development, how to best nurture curiosity, and how critically important this was in order to raise a successful, independent adult.

After I got married and had children of my own, I went out of my way with my sons to encourage them to try new things. If they found something interesting and exciting, then it was interesting and exciting to me too. When Vince started dancing as a child, I turned up the music and helped him discover new songs. I learned to let my kids try pretty much everything they wanted to try, and I let them explore every opportunity that came their way that wasn't sketchy or dangerous. Being well rounded is a gift that can open up so many doors in life.

While studying at Bethune-Cookman, I was also expanding my own horizons by getting my first off-campus job during my junior year. The college was located near the downtown Beach Street area of Daytona Beach, where most restaurants, banks, and department stores were located. The first big shopping mall in the Daytona area, the Volusia Mall, had not been built at that time, so downtown Daytona was still the main retail hub in town. My job was at the downtown Sears Roebuck department store, which later moved to the Mall after I stopped working there. I worked in the shoe department at Sears. Back before the internet, selling shoes was a common profession across America. You usually needed to go to a store if you wanted shoes, especially properly fitting shoes. A salesperson like me would then measure your foot and recommend the best-fit shoe. In my job I used one of those old-school sliding metal shoe size measuring devices. To this day, I think knowing how to accurately measure your own shoe size is a life skill.

Anyway, there was a young, handsome man, about five years older than me, who was the manager of a few departments next to the shoe department. We became friendly, and one day he asked me on a date. His name was Vincent Lennard Carter. Yup, Vince and Christopher's dad.

Vincent Lennard (he's technically not Vince Carter Sr., as they have different middle names) played football at Shaw University in his younger years and also came from a well-established local family, based in DeLand. He was a top local athlete, something of a legend back at DeLand High School, where he had been an accomplished multi-sport varsity athlete who excelled in both basketball and football.

Vince, the elder, and I got married after a few years of dating. After we were married, we soon started our family.

Getting married to someone who was an athlete provided my first real glimpse into the world of elite youth and high school sports. Vince's father's family, unlike mine, was a big sports family too. For them, sports were more a way of life, way more important than just something you watched on TV.

While my husband Vince was a great local high school athlete, his younger brother, Oliver Lee, was a state-wide phenomenon. In the mid-1970s, Oliver became the best basketball player in Volusia County and one of the very best in all of Florida. He was already being recruited by top NCAA programs too when I first met him.

Oliver played on the boys' basketball team for DeLand High School, about 40 miles from Daytona Beach. As Oliver grew to be around 6'7" in high school, he could play any basketball position, from point guard to center, but he preferred playing shooting guard or small forward—the same positions his nephew Vince would also favor some day. Vince and Oliver also share an uncanny resemblance and body build.

DeLand, Florida, and its high school were about a half hour drive from where my husband and I lived back then, so we tried to go to as many of Oliver's high school games as we could. I'll never forget trying to climb up the bleachers in the DeLand High School gym to watch Oliver play ball while I was at an advanced stage of my pregnancy with Vince. I was so pregnant and big! I recall struggling to climb the stairs to find a seat in the crowded gym. But I didn't mind; it was fun.

I didn't know it then, but being pregnant while climbing those stairs was the first of many personal sacrifices I was to make at the altar of basketball. Luckily, I had no idea how many more were on the way! I had no clue that one day I would structure my work, home life, and any vacation time around catering to the needs of an athlete like Oliver. Ignorance is sometimes bliss.

What I did know was that the raw home game basketball environment was a blast. I don't think I ever felt so connected to live sports before these high school games. Back in that DeLand gym in the mid-1970s, it was so electric—the bleachers packed with folks wearing those wild 1970s clothes, the big hair, the band playing fight songs, and Oliver's family, including my pregnant self, going crazy whenever he dunked the ball. As I said, Oliver was the spitting image of young Vince, and in retrospect it was like watching a living premonition.

I also glimpsed how Oliver was recruited by many big-name NCAA programs. He ultimately selected Marquette University, which was located pretty far away from us, in Milwaukee, Wisconsin. At the time, Marquette was an NCAA Division I powerhouse, under the supervision of its future Naismith Basketball Hall of Fame coach Al McGuire. In fact, during Oliver's senior year of high school, the Marquette Golden Eagles won the NCAA Championship Tournament and ended their incredible season as the number one men's college basketball team in America. You can only imagine how alluring Marquette's title championship run would have been to young Oliver, who watched it all happen on live

TV. I believe he'd already committed to play at Marquette when they won the title. (In an interesting side note, Marquette beat the University of North Carolina team to win its national title. The UNC Tar Heels were led by an eventual Hall of Fame coach, too—Dean Smith. More on him later, too.)

Oliver played four years at Marquette. Both my husband Vince and I were so proud of him, though this meant our road trips to see him play came to an end. We were now blessed to be able to watch Marquette play games on National TV, including four straight appearances in the NCAA Tournament. During Oliver's sophomore year, the Marquette Golden Eagles even made it to the Sweet Sixteen during the March Madness of the NCAA Tourney. Whenever given an opportunity to play, Oliver always balled out.

Al McGuire retired after his 1976–77 team won the championship, so Oliver was coached by new head coach Hank Raymonds. Every year, under the guidance of Coach Raymonds, Oliver improved his play, and was rewarded with more playing time. By his senior year, Oliver started all 31 games the Eagles played, and averaged nearly 18 points and 6.5 rebounds per game. These are quality player stats coming from an elite NCAA basketball program.

Believe it or not, from its inception until the mid-1980s, the NBA draft had ten rounds, instead of the two it has now. In the 1981 draft Oliver was selected #15 in the fourth round, #84 overall by the Chicago Bulls. He was so excited; we all were! But things changed quickly. Oliver dutifully attended the Bulls' training camp, but then his budding NBA career stalled out as quickly as it emerged. He sat on the Bulls bench briefly as a rookie, then was cut from the team. He never played in the NBA again.

Oliver had the physique (6'7", 215 lbs. when drafted), the determination, the drive, the college stats, the elite coaching, and the skill to play professional basketball. He was the best basketball player I had ever seen in person up to that point. So, what happened? Why was he cut? I never figured it out back then. I'm not sure one can retrospectively. I now know so much of pro sports and college sports can be politics. If you don't make a positive impression on the right coach at the right time, you may not be fully appreciated and your talents may be overlooked. You may not be fortunate to have the right mentors to grow your game the right way. The makeup of the roster also matters: is your position stacked on that team, or do they need your skills to compete now? There are so many other factors, but so much of it seemed to boil down to luck and connections. Which didn't seem fair.

I never forgot it. This made a real impression on me. My son, Vince, was born right before Oliver started at Marquette. While I was a young mother with Vince and his brother, Christopher, Oliver's journey gave me food for thought. His family all thought he was good enough to go pro. I believed it too, but I also remembered those great South Florida athletes who never made it to the pros. When Oliver was cut, I think this made me realize how truly difficult it was to make an NBA roster.

Perhaps now you can better understand why I was so skeptical about young Vince's potential to make it as a professional athlete, despite his obvious talent, and all the trophies he so easily won. But that was my honest reality. There was some real-life evidence behind my doubt. As a result, I never even considered raising Vince as though he'd be a basketball pro someday. I raised him with the goal that he'd be a huge success no matter what path and career he chose to pursue. I strongly recommend this approach.

3

Dunking in the Sixth Grade

Vincent Lamar Carter was born on January 26, 1977, in Daytona Beach, Florida at Halifax Hospital (now Halifax Medical Center). Given Vince's tall adult height (6'6"), you might think he would have been born a large baby, but he only weighed 6 lbs., 14 oz at birth and was 22 inches long from head to toe. His brother Christopher was born 2 years, 10 months later and weighed 2 oz more. They were both healthy, slightly below-average weight babies.

Vince held a Nerf basketball in his hands before he could even sit up without being in someone's lap or with a pillow being propped behind him. It was almost like the basketball chose him, like that Nerf ball was attached to his hand with Velcro. Although I found this odd, I just figured some kids like dolls or stuffed animals, and Vince just liked this puffy ball instead.

One afternoon in 1979, two-year-old Vincent was playing in his paternal grandmother's driveway with a full-sized regulation basketball and an adult-height hoop. He tossed the ball towards the hoop in a determined attempt to make the basket. He missed over and over. I vividly recall that when he did not get the success he sought, he flopped down on the driveway and began to cry. Sitting in the lawn chair keeping a close eye on him, I told him, "Get up, stop crying, and keep trying. You'll get it." Thus encouraged, Vincent got up, brushed away the little dirt that had gotten on his leg, and began to toss the ball again. I began, intermittently, taking a few shots with a Polaroid instant camera. Lo and behold, he made a basket! At first, I did not believe what I saw through the camera lens. The photo shot out of the Polaroid, and after a few seconds of fanning it, I saw the proof. He had made the basket!

Some parents might have interpreted a two-year-old making a grown-up basket as a sign of future athletic greatness. A future NBA calling. But I did not take it this way. I saw it as a sign of determination. I knew determined people got places in life. I liked what I saw in baby Vincent but did not overinterpret it.

As Vincent grew older, he seemingly always had a real or imaginary basketball in his hands. At approximately three years old Vince was sleeping with a Nerf basketball beside him. Seriously, he would have it next to him like it was his teddy bear. As a young mother, I wasn't sure what to do about this. The Nerf ball was soft and puffy, so it wasn't surprising Vince had treated it like a doll. But at around seven years old, Vince began sleeping with a full-sized basketball in his bed. So I tried to stop it. I'd gently push the ball to the other side of the bed away from him. It didn't seem normal. What was wrong with his Winnie-the-Pooh? He didn't care. He just wanted to be next to that ball. He'd bring the ball right back to himself for a cuddle. Now, my mom, Peggy, wouldn't have stood for any of this basketball-in-the-bed nonsense! She would have put a stop to it—you likely know by now that I'm not kidding. But even as a young mother, I was already diverging from my mom's absolutist ways. I merely politely asked Vince not to do it, then switched the ball out with one of his stuffed animals. I put the ball on his dresser. So then he tried to hide it. Imagine thinking you could hide a full-sized basketball under the covers, and that no one would notice this massive round lump tucked next to you under the sheets and blanket! Back when I was fully pregnant with Vince, struggling to climb those bleacher stairs back at the DeLand gym, I showed less than that basketball in his bed did! So, what did I do? I made a parental judgment call and decided to respect his determination and object of affection. My own mom never would have given in. Never. That ball would have gone out with the trash. But I wasn't my mom and it seemed harmless, if weird. I let him have his way. Again, some ambitious sports parents would have taken this as a sign of future basketball destiny; I merely found it annoying.

This was just the start of Vince's pure love of the game. If he did not have access to a basketball, he would appear to be dribbling and crossing-over with an imaginary one. It seemed every place in our house and yard could serve as a basketball half court for Vince's phantom ball handling skills. It was sure something to watch. Sometimes, it looked like he was possessed. Interestingly, while researching this book, I spoke with some of Vince's former youth and college coaches, and I discovered that Vincent was known for miming basketball moves throughout his entire early life, whenever he didn't have a ball. He didn't care how it looked, even if he looked like some damn mime. I also heard stories about how, when he actually held a real basketball but had no court to play on, Vince still found a way to practice. Both his high school and college coaches remembered that, if left alone, Vince would do ball spinning drills on his own, and even play catch-and-shoot off their office walls. Vince wasn't just doing random drills either. According to some accomplished coaches, he was methodically trying to improve his ball spin and control. He didn't care if it was the head coach's office; he'd do his thing!

He did his thing all the time back at our house too, of

course, but I'd gotten so used to it, it became normal. I must confess that, for decades, I seriously thought he only did these solitary practice moves around his family. I knew he did the spin drills in his bedroom—where he spun the ball off his fingertips as high up as he could, then caught it and spun it again. He'd done that drill at home since he could pick up the ball. But the catch-and-shoot off the walls in the coach's office was a new one for me. He did not try that at home. I would have heard that while trying to go to sleep, and it would have triggered my inner Peggy. Child Vince, apparently, could detect my limits. Now, I really wonder if he would have felt this free to learn his ball sense and practice his game anywhere if I had forced him not to sleep with the basketball. Or told him not to do his spin, catch, and mime moves in the house. It's curious how the little things you do as a parent eventually add up.

    I didn't know I had a future basketball phenomenon in the making. Basketball wasn't Vince's first team sport. He may have fallen in love with the ball, but I wasn't pushing the sport on him. Like many small children in the USA, Vincent's first team sport was soccer. He was 5 years old when he joined his first team. Back then, there wasn't the same elite youth sports infrastructure that exists today. There weren't that many famous sports academies, or super-team Amateur Athletic Union (AAU) programs.

    At the start, everything was local, straightforward, and affordable. I signed Vince up for a kids' soccer league and team at our local rec (recreation) center. Soccer proved to be a fun way for Vince to begin to learn what it was like to be a good member of a team; to learn how to work with others for a common cause—to win the game. Even at the age of 5, Vincent showed advanced athleticism, and he was already noticeably taller than other kids his age. He wasn't very fast, however; little kids who are taller can be more awkward at running. It's a rule I witnessed with both my sons and with other tall kids. I call it "the Rabbit vs. Giraffe problem." The giraffe, having a much higher center of gravity and spindly legs, can't take off running like the rabbit whose body is much lower to the ground and whose legs are built like a spring. Once the giraffe gets going, however, it can get up to a full gallop. Tall kids like Vince were kind of like those giraffes at first. But I assure you they eventually grow out of the awkward phase and find their proper balance. One day they will be rabbits, too!

Even if he was the best athlete on that first soccer team, Vince still understood that he needed his teammates to know they made contributions to the "W" too. His instincts guided him to set his teammates up for easy scores. He loved assisting goals. I don't remember ever teaching him to actively involve his teammates; he just knew he needed to involve them to win. He always respected and appreciated his teammates, even when they weren't very good. But whenever it became obvious they couldn't score a goal, Vincent was never shy about getting the job done himself. It was clear that this youngster liked the feeling of winning the game most of all, which is important in sports.

Sometimes I ruffle feathers now among my friends and family when I say that for athletics, I don't believe in participation awards for all the kids. You can give every kid a certificate or ribbon for participating on a team for a season, of course. They earned that. But I'm not in favor of getting a ribbon or medal for just showing up to a tournament or game. The point of sports is to win! I communicated this idea to Vince many times growing up, and I recommend you do so, too. Yes, sports teach leadership and friendship-building skills—great; but winning is still the point. Looking back, I'm grateful Vince started sports before the participating certificates were a thing, because I might have had words with his coaches about that.

Now, even if I taught him winning was important, I don't remember teaching him to *love* winning, exactly. I don't think you can teach that. He just did. I suspect if you instill that need to win in your kids, in a positive way, then the love of winning will probably follow. But, no matter what, *don't ever shame your child for losing*—instead, help them make a plan for how they're going to win the next time. Help make your little athlete more ambitious. Figure out together the practical skills they need to work on to improve. Help them figure out how to make their teammates better, too.

Again, Vince was always a great teammate. In today's elite AAU basketball world, this isn't always the case with star players, even though elite players who make personal sacrifices for the team are always in great demand in college ball and the NBA. These players are often referred to as "glue guys," because they fill in the gaps and lapses in team defense and offense. Vince's willingness to do the little things on court, particularly on defense and mentoring younger players, helped prolong his career. The benefits of being a good team player last a lifetime. You'll have a lot more real friends, too.

At seven years old, in 1984, Vince finally joined his first basketball team. As you may have gathered, Vince had already done everything he could on his own to become proficient in the sport. In addition to miming basketball moves and sleeping next to the ball for moral support, he also spent hours a day practicing shots on our driveway hoop. He was showing off his handles dribbling the ball up and down sidewalks and at the local playground courts.

Vincent began to play organized basketball with the Volusia County recreation leagues. Of course no one knew it, but this was the beginning of what proved to be a stellar career in the sport. It honestly didn't occur to me that I was introducing a "ringer" into the local rec leagues, but I kind of did. As you might imagine, he advanced in the leagues quickly.

While Vince was mastering his handles, his home life was changing. His father and I had issues, then separated, and then finally divorced when Vince was seven years old. I'm not going to dwell on my marriage situation too much,

Dunking in the Sixth Grade

but this drastically changed my outlook on life, and my responsibilities. Before the divorce, I was working in private industry, at a job at the Brunswick Corporation, which was a defense contractor that had an office in DeLand, Florida. I worked on the business side of things, doing human resources administrative work. Although I enjoyed working at Brunswick, shortly after Vince was born I began teaching business subjects. As mentioned already, my mom wanted to make sure I had that teaching degree to fall back on, and I have to admit that sometimes my mom was right about things, including the benefits of a teaching career. Suddenly, those summers off, and winter and spring breaks, looked really appealing. So I started looking around for a teaching job.

Meanwhile, Vince continued to hoop. In 1986, at 9 years of age, Vincent set a new scoring record at the Port Orange, FL, rec center, scoring 31 points in a youth basketball game. Recently, a few longtime residents of the city told me that this record has not yet been broken.

Basketball wasn't all that Vince did. He loved music and began learning to play instruments, including percussion, baritone and saxophone. He learned how to read music. Like me, he loved to dance, too. Whenever his cousin, Tiffany, was in town, she, Vince, and Chris, would frequently hold dance-offs together. Apparently, they also loved reenacting moves from the world of professional wrestling. Back in the 80s, the kids would watch WWE (World Wrestling Entertainment) matches on TV, then wrestle each other off from the upstairs balcony, landing on the couch below, in imitation of the TV competitors. I would have been furious had I known about this potentially dangerous activity back then, but I did not. I also don't know how that poor couch survived!

While young Vince excelled at local rec league basketball, I found my first teaching job at Deltona Junior High School. So, what kind of business education classes did junior high school kids need? The answer was simple back then: typing. As readers over a certain age will recall, the most important business machine in America before computers was the IBM Selectric. This was the typewriter used by most businesses for several decades, and it was the typical one used in schools as well. At my school, we had a classroom with rows of typewriters, similar to the computer classrooms of today.

Teaching typing was fun—in part, because it was an elective, so everybody in the class wanted to be there more or less. Typing students were typically kids who either wanted to work as business secretaries (now called administrative assistants) some day, or kids who planned on going to college and needed to learn how to type up their school papers and applications. I enjoyed teaching everyone. Vince, meanwhile, kept the local rec league on its toes.

About this time, I moved to Ormond Beach, Florida. This was a significant move. Again, looking back, I'm trying to recognize some of the decisions I made that helped mold Vince into who he is today. One of my key decisions that contributed to Vince's athletic development back then was simply choosing to live at a safe biking distance away from the local rec center—though I didn't understand how important this would be to Vince's development until later. At the time, it just seemed convenient and healthy.

After my divorce, our new home in Ormond Beach had a bike and walking trail all the way from our house to the rec center. Vince, his brother Christopher, and their cousin Tiffany, when she came to visit, could easily bike over to the rec center, where there was always an adult coach supervising the kids in the gym after school, on weekends, and during daytime summer hours. I remember one such coach the kids all loved, named "Stretch" because he was as tall as a tree and had been a college basketball player himself. Because the kids could bike on the trails on their own, to and from the rec center, I was often not present when Vince practiced basketball in the rec center gym. My niece Tiffany, who was often present, recently told me that she was convinced back then that Vince already had what it took to go pro some day. She swears everyone else in the gym believed it, too. According to Tiffany, Vince frequently played pickup basketball games with bigger kids, and even grown men, and was usually the best player on the court. Even though I did start to learn through friends and acquaintances about Vince balling out at the rec center, my background watching his uncle's experience with the NBA still made me very skeptical about his chances as a pro.

Around this time, I went to teach at Campbell Junior High School, in Daytona Beach not far from Bethune-Cookman. This was an important move for me for many reasons, and this is the school where I taught during Vince's own middle school and high school years. While I was transitioning to my new job, Vince's athletic talent was starting to attract even more attention. People were coming up to me at school or at church and telling me they heard my son was a baller.

Vince was still a small child, so while this was flattering, it also seemed premature. But then one day someone told me Vince could already dunk the ball. I don't remember the exact day or month, but I do remember Vince was in the sixth grade. One day everyone was buzzing about a local elementary school kid that could legit dunk the ball. I'm not sure if I figured out this was Vince, or if my friend who told me already figured it out. Either way, I realized not only that Vince could dunk, but also that he didn't feel the need to brag about it or tell me about it. He learned how to do it because *he* wanted to do it. I remember being proud of him, not only for being able to dunk, but also because he was achieving his goals—metaphorical and literal—through his own determination and persistence. He did not feel like he had to brag about it to his family or friends. He let his actions speak louder than his words, which is a great life habit.

So later that day, after school, I asked Vince about the

dunk. He told me he wanted to surprise me by dunking next time I visited the court with him—which he did, a few days later; and his plan worked: I was amazed he could dunk in sixth grade. I still did not predict an NBA career for my child, but I did start to realize he possessed special athletic gifts. I also realized he might have the skill to make the varsity team in high school.

That's where my dreams for him stopped. I didn't even dream about him making it to college ball, yet. He was still so young and still trying new things. He excelled in most activities that he tried, and I wanted to make sure he developed as many talents as possible. No matter how good at sports he was, school still came first.

4

Volleyball, Football, Basketball… Band?

Education was always the priority in the Carter household, as Vince was born into a family of generational educators. My most important "house rule" was *No Grades, No Play*. In our home, we put a lot of weight upon the term "student-athlete." A youngster is a student first, then an athlete.

In Florida, the minimum grade point average (g.p.a.) that a student must maintain to play sports or be involved in any school extracurricular activity is 2.0. In the Carter household, the minimum grade point average was 3.0. No exceptions. In addition, Vincent was required to get involved in other school interests besides basketball. We didn't want him to grow up only knowing sports.

As we know, sometimes children don't follow the rules or measure up to their parents' expectations. In other words, they get into trouble. When our house rules were violated, even before I became a single mom, I was most often the parent that would levy punishment. Thankfully, I rarely had occasion to do this. But when punishment was deemed necessary I had another extremely important rule: punishment would never be discussed or levied on game day. Whether the punishment was not being allowed to watch TV, or go to the rec center, or even the rare spanking, it could wait. I wanted Vincent to walk into competitions with a positive mindset and focus, and a good vibe. There was never anything he did wrong that was so grave that my response could not wait until later, to whatever I deemed an appropriate time. This also gave me time to reflect and understand my own intentions. Life tip: think before you reward or punish. What are your positive intentions with punishment or rewards? What positive outcome is the goal? If you can't answer these simple questions, at minimum, you probably shouldn't be punishing anyone.

A few years after my divorce, while teaching at Campbell Junior High School, I began dating a teacher at the school. This was Harry Robinson, who was the band director and music teacher. Harry made learning to play an instrument fun for students. After a few years of dating, Harry and I got married, and Vince got his very own bonus dad. The boys called him "Pops." They adored Harry, and vice versa.

In the fifth grade, Vincent began taking saxophone lessons. Harry got Vincent started, then hired his peer band directors to continue the tutoring. As parents, we acted on the same premise as frequently influences parents whose children are learning to drive—get them started yourself, but let someone else do the work of teaching them the skill fully.

Vincent enjoyed music and strove to learn to play as many instruments as he could. Eventually, he learned to play the saxophone, baritone and trumpet, as well as being a pretty good percussionist. By his senior year of high school, Vincent was voted to be the drum major of the Mainland High School Marching Band (Daytona Beach, FL). Throughout his high school years, I thought Vince might very well end up with a career in music, maybe as a music teacher like Harry.

Vincent was very popular in both middle school and high school. He always had a pleasant demeanor and was kind and engaging. He just had that "people person" thing going on. He liked everybody, and everybody liked him. He was a member of the Homecoming Court and participated in the Fellowship of Christian Athletes, Student Government and the Remote-Control Club or "RC-Club" which was basically a club for kids who liked to have fun with remote-controlled vehicles like toy cars, boats and airplanes. It was a fairly nerdy pursuit, and Vince loved every minute of being a nerd!

With regard to sports, Vince started to separate from the pack relatively early. He was obviously gifted as an athlete. When a high school student is a stellar athlete or, in the view of coaches, has a high ceiling, they are going to be highly sought after, as indeed was true in Vince's case from middle school onward.

If parents don't create limits, coaches will have the athlete playing every sport offered on campus. Things got a little dicey when Vincent became extremely involved in high school campus sports and the coaches kept coming. Besides basketball and band, Vincent played volleyball and football. As a high school freshman, he showed a lot of promise as a quarterback. He played quarterback through his high school freshman year. Fortunately for the Carter household schedule, the freshman football games would be played on Mondays through Thursdays, which left Vince free to participate in the high school marching band at the pre-game and half-time of the varsity football games. Vincent wanted to continue with music and knew that it was expected of him to do so, because, again, we wanted him to be well rounded.

One afternoon, I was on the Mainland High School campus waiting for band practice to begin. I was the band announcer during the four years that Vincent was in the band, and for several years thereafter. To kill a little time, I walked into the gym and watched the boys' volleyball practice. I watched the drills that Coach Lenny Carr was conducting, which seemed to strengthen the players' legs and increase their jumping ability. Even though Vince had been dunking since the sixth grade, I could immediately sense that this drill, and some others from Coach Carr, might benefit him. That night, at dinner, I offered a challenge to Vincent. Sneakily, I prefaced it by mentioning the importance of making a difference and leading the way at school. Then I asked him to consider getting a couple of his friends to try out with him for the volleyball team. I wasn't trying to develop Vince into a super athlete, I just knew that if he learned how to jump in a more expert way, he'd probably be less likely to be injured in the contact sports he played.

Vincent took me up on my challenge. Again, I didn't play fair—I knew he couldn't resist a challenge! He sure didn't resist this one. He played on the volleyball team his sophomore and junior years. Both years, he was honored with the title of Volusia County Boys Volleyball Player-of-the-Year. Despite this, Vince stopped playing at the end of his junior year so that he could focus on basketball during his senior year.

Given the eagerness of the high school coaches to have students of superior athletic ability on their teams, it didn't take long before the track and field coaches tried to recruit Vince to try the high jump. They were always talking up their squad to him, and even challenging him a little to try to jump. It finally worked. One day, when Mainland was hosting a track and field event, Vincent decided at the last minute that he would try it. This was a county-wide meet, and he did not have time to practice or even purchase the proper footwear. He tried it anyway and came away with a county meet award for the best high jump, winning this award in his basketball shoes! After that, I knew Vince wanted to join their team, too, but he simply did not have enough free time. Already our schedules were overwhelmed. This was before Vince could drive, so Harry or I had to drive him everywhere. His schedule was already packed weeks in advance, and we could barely keep up this frenetic pace. I learned another life lesson—that by the time the elite student-athlete reaches his or her sophomore year, there is one big transformative decision that will need to be made: which sport to specialize in.

Nowadays, kids seemingly specialize in sports at a young age. I don't think this is a good idea. If Vince hadn't played soccer, his footwork probably would not have developed so naturally. If he hadn't played football, he'd probably have been more afraid of in-game contact, and his hand-eye coordination might not have been so exemplary. Volleyball made Vince an expert at jumping and landing the right way. Any elite basketball coach knows proper post-dunk landing technique is one of the hardest things to teach and to become good at. Not specializing in basketball early was one of the smartest things Vince ever did.

For the Carter household, the major decision for Vincent, which was made after his sophomore year, was which sport he should play in college: basketball or football. Vince had tremendous arm strength, as well as high-level running and passing ability. He was already leading the JV football team to wins. But it had become a real challenge keeping all the coaches and the band director happy. Coaches tend to be quite territorial, and when a student-athlete is on their team, that's "their player". This attitude can limit student-athletes from homing in on what works best for them.

Although the student-athlete should play an integral role in making his scheduling work, I believe parents should take the lead. I didn't think Vince should continue to play both football and basketball. I could not see the viability of him dealing with the pressure of being a two-sport student athlete while maintaining a respectable grade point average.

Complicating things was the fact that one of Vince's college sports heroes at the time was Florida State's Charlie Ward, who was one of the best two-sport college athletes of all time. As the Florida State University (FSU) star quarterback, Charlie won college football's Heisman Award—he was that good. He would easily have been selected in the first round of the NFL draft. But Charlie, instead, chose to play pro basketball, his other varsity college sport at FSU. He was selected #26 in the NBA draft by the Knicks and had a fine career in the League.

I'm pretty sure Vince thought he could be like Charlie, but I thought this might be too ambitious. Even if Vince could play two college sports, what was the point? I wanted Vince to have every opportunity to enjoy college and not feel enormous pressure all the time. I explained to him he would have no free time, and a reduced social life, if he played two sports, while maintaining a respectable g.p.a. During several family discussions, we brought up the pros and cons of each sport. The decision, however, was ultimately his. He chose his first love, basketball. Once this decision was made, the stress of negotiating with coaches so that Vince could attend overlapping practices for basketball, band, volleyball, and football was somewhat relieved.

In 1991, when Vince was 14, there was already a lot of hype surrounding him before he even started high school, particularly relating to the fact he could already dunk. Meanwhile, for decades, Mainland had a reputation for grooming outstanding athletes in several sports. Because of this there was an enormous grass roots fan base for the school's football and basketball teams. My concern was that Vince was being hyped before he had even tried out for the basketball team. Fans were prematurely predicting wins before he was even on the team!

Prior to being on the high school team, Vincent had several skilled coaches who had volunteered through the various recreation leagues. Jerry Williams was one of his elementary school coaches whom I remember fondly. The late Coach Earl Griggs was his junior high school coach, who gave him a firm foundation in the sport.

Just as Vincent was entering the eighth grade, however,

Volusia County Schools went from the junior high to the middle school concept. With this change, middle schools did not engage in competitive sports. This was like a wrench thrown into our plans. At that point Vince had clearly outgrown the local rec league, and we were counting on him continuing to develop his basketball skills at school. Suddenly, however, we needed a developmental plan B. We found the answer in AAU Basketball. So that Vincent would not have any break in his development as a young basketball player while at middle school, we signed him up for an elite AAU team in Orlando, Florida.

AAU stands for Amateur Athletic Union, and it's an organization in the United States that oversees a nationwide system of amateur leagues and tournaments in a number of sports. It's similar to Little League for baseball, except that AAU covers many sports, including basketball, volleyball, golf, bowling, and dozens more. Currently, AAU is a really big deal in youth basketball. There are AAU clubs and teams for every level of play, but it's the elite AAU basketball teams that get most of the attention.

When Vince was a teenager, there were already elite AAU teams, but it was not the enormous, high-profile industry it is today. Nowadays there are three elite AAU "shoe circuits" or leagues, run by Nike, Adidas, and Under Armour. Within each of these elite circuits are individual teams led by top coaches, trainers, and even some former and current NBA players. There are big-name independent AAU clubs outside the shoe circuits too, like the popular Overtime Elite and many others. Elite AAU teams are considered to be the "feeder" system for both top NCAA basketball programs and the NBA, especially via its developmental G League. Not only do elite AAU tournaments attract top college coaches and pro scouts, but highlights from these events also generate hundreds of thousands of views on YouTube and other social media.

Back in the early 1990s, things were very different. AAU

teams and tournaments did not yet have a high profile. They were known amongst elite coaches and scouts, but not so much to the public. These AAU clubs and teams made money by charging parents for coaching, practice time, uniforms, travel costs, and tournament fees. Enrolling your child on one of these teams wasn't cheap.

Vince's Orlando AAU team, SOYSA, was coached by the late Earl Graham, who was very capable. We were lucky to have him mentor Vince. Having Vincent play on this team, however, required a tremendous parental commitment. After my day ended as a business instructor, I transported Vincent two days a week to basketball practice. This trek to Orlando was a round trip of approximately 120 miles. The AAU basketball tournaments were on the weekend, when Vince's bonus dad, Harry, took the wheel. That meant a third weekly trip to Orlando, or other parts of Florida.

This went on for Vincent's entire eighth grade year. Dinner was a stop at various restaurants on the way home. Real restaurants that offered real nutritious food. We didn't do fast food. I tried to make sure Vince always ate at restaurants that served vegetables and meat dishes like you'd get at home. Homestyle buffet restaurants were Vince's favorite, because I swear that boy could eat! Watching him and his brother scarf down food at a buffet was like having a front row seat at one of those competitive eating contests you see on TV.

Vince completed his homework in the car on the way to, and if necessary, back from, practice. Though taxing, this was a good experience for Vincent. It helped him develop a valuable life skill. Once in college, Vince would do his college homework on the plane, too. In the NBA, he'd watch game film or read scouting reports about competitor teams during team flights. Being able to multi-task and make use of time spent traveling is a real asset to an elite athlete every step of the way.

The players on Vince's first AAU team were from all around

the greater Orlando area and presented a much higher skill level than our local kids. For the first time ever, Vince came face-to-face with some of the best young basketball talent in Florida. This was eye opening for Vince, and for me as well. Skills-wise, Vince fit in immediately, but he didn't dominate the floor for once, like he did in the local rec leagues.

The coaches in Orlando continually praised Vincent's work ethic, basketball sense, and athletic ability. But they did that for other elite players on the team too. Vince still wanted to be the best, to be special. Now he started to understand how much effort and practice this would take. I think that AAU team was kind of a reality check for him; it made him realize, from age 14, how hard he'd have to work to be the elite amongst the basketball elite.

It made me realize how hard a journey he'd have before him, too. But unlike Vincent, who was probably daydreaming about becoming an NBA pro already, I didn't have any illusions. I was still thinking his future was: college, education, professional degrees.

But Vince wanted to get better, so another parental sacrifice was made. Vince started to receive invitations to exclusive national basketball camps. These were not like normal sports summer camps. These were invitation-only events featuring the best youth basketball players and/or teams in the country. This was the pathway for Vince to be scouted by the best college scouts in America, and to see where he stood against the best competition.

As an educator, every spring I had a week's vacation, also known as Spring Break. I love cruises, so that was my typical treat to myself—sailing around tropical islands on a luxury liner, far away from the classroom and students. Financially, however, it was not possible for me to go on cruises *and* for Vincent to go to prestigious basketball camps. So, what happened? You guessed it. I stopped cruising and Vincent started out-of-state basketball camping. Vince also began attending camps whenever he had a break from school, either individually or with his Mainland team, including during summers and winter holiday break.

Vince's camps included University of Cincinnati, Beach Ball Classic (Myrtle Beach, SC), Magic Johnson Roundball Classic (Detroit, MI), Five Star in Pennsylvania, and Nike Camp (Chicago, IL). Most of these camps still exist and continue to showcase the best young players in basketball. Almost all North American NBA stars attended at least some of them.

Via the experience of these camps, the AAU teams, and his high school team, Vince emerged on the national basketball radar. In the state and national rankings Vincent was a perennial top five selection. It was worth sacrificing my cruises and some family time to give us a clear picture of how he measured up amongst other outstanding players in the country.

The summer before Vincent's high school junior year, he was invited to play with an AAU team, Playaz, in Patterson, New Jersey. This team was coached by Jimmy Salmon. One might ask, how does a basketball player from Florida end up on an AAU team in New Jersey? Once an athlete begins to appear on the various sports publications rankings list, and to participate in camps around the country, then the AAU, college/university, and even private high school coaches begin to court them. Before the internet and cell phones, this was done by sending flyers to players and their coaches, and sometimes making phone calls.

A lot of research is required to understand not only the reputation of the coach, but also how that coach is in practice. What works for one athlete may not work for others. Serious family discussions should take place concerning your child's desires and what makes the most sense for your family.

Coaches use contrasting approaches, have various temperaments, and interact with players differently. To be successful, student-athletes must develop their personal

Vincent at age 7(left) and (right) at Port Orange, FL, Recreation Basketball at the same age. (Carter family photo collection)

Vincent at Port Orange, FL, Recreation Basketball, age 9. (Carter family photo collection)

Vincent as safety patrol in the fifth grade.

The Making of Vince Carter

Vincent in the Mainland High School Band, Daytona Beach, FL, age 15.

Vincent as a Mainland High School Band Drum Major, 1994/95.

Volleyball, Football, Basketball... Band?

Vince Carter playing for the Mainland Buccaneers, FL, sporting his favored jersey number 15.

Vincent in tenth grade in his volleyball team T-shirt and cap.

The Making of Vince Carter

October 2, 1994

Mr. Vince Carter
7 Nottingham
 Drive
Ormand Beach, FL   32174

Dear Vince,

    I trust your school year is progressing nicely. I am sure you are staying busy with your involvement in the band, basketball and all the time that the home visits must have occupied. I imagine you are ready for the break that the October recruiting deadline provides.

    We are two days away from the beginning of our training camp. The excitement and expectations of the NBA season are rampant in San Antonio right now. This year should provide a wealth of success for our team.   That same enthusiasm must be present at Mainland for your upcoming season.

    Vince, I was fortunate to coach Danny Manning at the University of Kansas. I have maintained a very close relationship with both he and his family, and we often reflect on Danny's high school career and the recruiting process. Both he and his parents speak of the pressure that faces not only you but your entire family. It is very important for you to rely heavily on their support and to always express yourself to them. Through this open communication, you will be able to reach the best college selection for you. Vince Carter is going to be a great basketball player no matter where he goes. An important consideration should be "Where can I be the happiest as a student?" Maintaining the support that

(Above and opposite) Letter from R C Buford of San Antonio Spurs during the college recruitment process. (Carter family collection)

has led to your success to this point, will be important to achieving even greater successes in the future. Danny also relates that he enjoyed his Senior year of high school much more because he made his selection early.

As I approach my new position in player-personnel, I get to study many future draft projections. On more than one occasion, your name has been mentioned. NBA scouting services will be following you closely over the next few years. This will be a very exciting time. Looking at the NBA draft in recent years, the influence of underclassmen is very strong. Without de-emphasizing your education, at some point a player of your abilities will be faced with the decision whether to enter the draft early. The opportunity to really expand your talents and showcase your abilities within a comfortable personal setting should weigh heavily in your selection process. All the schools you are considering give you this latitude; some better than others. Good luck with this exciting decision. I regret that I will not be in Florida to watch your team. Hopefully I can get to Florida to see you play at some point this year.

Please give my best to your parents and to Chris. If you are ever near a Spurs game, please come and be my guest. Coach Kruger and McCullum both told me how much they enjoyed their home visit and the chance to see you recently.

Most Sincerely,

R.C. Buford
Director of Scouting

Alamodome   100 Montana   San Antonio, Texas 78203   (210) 554-7700   Fax (210) 554-7701

The Making of Vince Carter

THE UNIVERSITY OF NORTH CAROLINA

Basketball Office

P.O. Box 2126
Chapel Hill, NC 27515

or

Smith Center— Bowles Drive
Chapel Hill, NC 27514

Telephone (919) 962-1154

Dean E. Smith

Head Basketball Coach

Assistants:

Bill Guthridge
Phil Ford, Jr.
Dave Hanners

April 25, 1994

Mr. Vince Carter c/o Coach Charlie Brinkerhoff Daytona Beach Mainland High School
125 South Clyde—Morris Boulevard Daytona Beach, FL 32114

Dear Vince:

My assistant coach, Bill Guthridge, returned to Chapel Hill last week indicating how impressed he was in observing your workout. We both are excited that you may have an interest in The University of North Carolina as you seek academic and athletic balance in your college experience.

You surely appear to be the type of excellent student-athlete that we need for the freshman class entering in September of 1995. I look forward to coming to Daytona Beach during the July recruiting period to show our high interest in you, as well as watch you play. We do think you would enjoy our style of play at Chapel Hill,

Academically, The University of North Carolina is one of the top 25 universities in the nation with any poll you choose to use. Fortunately, many of our undergraduate departments are ranked among the very best in the United States. With your academic record you, undoubtedly, will look at this closely.

Additionally, we are located in a college town that many publications have listed as a most desirable place to live.
Illustrated called it the "perfect college town, and we have had many other compliments about this unique village. I did want to point out the environment here, as well as our academic reputation.

I do look forward to seeing you play in July and then visiting with you by telephone once it is legal. Of course, we can visit in the homes beginning sometime in September, and we hope to be included in your list of schools for home contacts.

(Above and opposite) Personal letter from the late Dean E. Smith, seeking to recruit Vince to the University of North Carolina (UNC)— which he succeeded in doing. (Carter family collection)

April 25, 1994 Mr. Vince Carter

Page 2

Coach Guthridge indicated that your parents are schoolteachers. This is impressive to me and to Coach Phil Ford, since we grew up in homes where our mothers and fathers were teachers. Even though you deserve credit being a tremendous young man and an outstanding student-athlete, I know you give credit to your parents as well.

I look forward to meeting you and your parents.

Warm regards to all.

Sincerely,

Dean Smith

Dean E. Smith

DES/rk cc: Coach Charlie Brinkerhoff

Vince —
Hope Brad Daugherty hasn't been too tough on you when you were younger! Now that we are recruiting you, Brad has to be careful about the NCAA rules. —

August 24, 1994.

Dear Vince:

Advanced Tiny, Band, Basketball, Volleyball and Great Kid! I can't wait to come down on the 12th or the 13th of September to visit with you. I am sure Duke would be perfect for you.

Take care,
Coach K

1991 & 1992 NCAA National Champions
Cameron Indoor Stadium • Box 90556 • Durham, N.C. 27708-0556 • Phone: 919/684-3777 • FAX 919/684-2489

(Right) A brief, but well informed, note from "Coach K" (Mike Krzyzewski), one of the college coaches who sought to recruit Vince. (Carter family collection)

The Making of Vince Carter

> July 8, 1994
>
> Dear Vince,
>
> I returned from Wisconsin this morning and wanted to write this note to thank you for arranging your workout. As I related to you via the telephone I was extremely impressed with your skills at this relatively young age. Some things are obvious but I also noted your leadership and your basketball "savvy"! A smart player like you always does well at Carolina and enjoys the way we play.
>
> (over)

> (2)
>
> I'll try to "catch" your All-Star Game on the 17th of July and then return to Daytona Beach to show our immense interest after the 17th and before July 30.
>
> We enjoyed seeing your family and look forward to visiting by telephone and then "in person" when the rules allow this.
>
> It is our hope that you will be with us for your college experience. You would enjoy it, I believe!
>
> Sincerely,
> Dean Smith

(Above and below) Personal letters from the late Dean E. Smith of UNC. (Carter family collection)

> Nov. 22, 1994
>
> Dear Vince,
>
> Enjoyed our visit by telephone last evening. I was pleased to talk with your Mom and Dad also. I know you are looking forward to tomorrow night and the first game. Hope it is a great start for you and the team as you move to the State Championship!
>
> Your Mother told me you will have Thanksgiving Dinner

> (2)
>
> with your grandmother while they are in Louisiana. Eat well and take good care of Chris!
>
> I did check on the score with Athletes in Action. We had them 82-32 with 13:08 left to play while winning 102-66. I heard Florida beat them by 5 points. Our Scramble defense was a huge difference since we forced 28 turnovers. You would like to play our Scramble and you would make many steals! (And dunks)
>
> I'm enclosing a copy of the letter that was lost at the high school during the storm. (Addressed wrong)
>
> Will call next week! Happy Thanksgiving,
> Sincerely, Dean Smith

48

methods of dealing with different styles of coaching, while being open to learning and still retaining the ability to enjoy the game. All of Vince's coaches had very different methods of coaching, and I believed he learned new skills from every one of them. The variety definitely benefited him.

  Even though Vince's participation in AAU was way more expensive than the local rec league, and a significant time commitment for all of us, I realized it was probably a good investment. It was making Vince a better player and putting him on the map of college scouts. Best of all, he was having fun. He was also going to start his high school basketball career from the best position possible, and he was so excited to finally start high school ball. It was quite the journey.

The Making of Vince Carter

5

The Quest for the State Championship

A freshman getting an immediate place, not to mention a starter, on a high school varsity team is unusual in any sport. I knew Vince had a real chance of achieving it, while our local community had already assigned him to lead the varsity squad in their minds. Vince's abilities were talked up in our community for a long time before he ever tried out for the team. Some local basketball fans were already convinced that Vince would lead Mainland High School to the basketball district championship and way beyond that. I think Vince enjoyed hearing the lofty sports gossip about himself, but I wasn't having any of it. I told him, "Don't buy into the hype. You have to try out for the team first."

I later learned that Vince's eventual Mainland High School coach, Charles Brinkerhoff, wasn't buying into the hype either, at first. Coach Brink was the Junior Varsity (JV) coach back then, and he thought that no matter how good this kid was—he hadn't seen Vince play in person yet—he'd benefit from being on the JV squad first, to improve his fundamentals. Coach Brink believed strongly in the fundamentals.

Then, he saw Vince at the team tryouts and realized that, well, no, maybe this kid *was* good enough to go straight to the varsity team. Coach Brink is an excellent judge of talent.

As a 14-year-old freshman, Vince was a six-foot tall, wiry young man. In those days, most youngsters who played basketball wanted to wear number 23—Michael Jordan's number. Vincent wanted that number too. But being the rookie freshman on the team, he figured there was no way that he was going to get Jordan's number. I told him, "Pick a number, and you make that number famous". The number he selected was 15. Number 15 served him well.

What didn't serve him well at first, however, was the size of his first varsity jersey. Remember, Vince went to a public high school back then, not some fancy private school, so custom jerseys with your last name sewn on the back were not a thing. What you got instead was a jersey worn by whichever boy was number 15 last season. One from which the last boy's sweat stains could be removed. Vince's first varsity uniform didn't fit him at all. It was more like a small tent than a jersey, as Vince's body hadn't filled out yet. It drooped off his shoulders, and there was so much excess fabric that he could get an updraft of wind puffing out the back of that jersey like a parachute if he ran too fast. I went to Mainland basketball head coach Richard "Dick" Toth and asked if I could have the uniform's seams taken in a bit to fit Vince better. Coach Toth seemed confused by my question, and politely explained that the jersey would be reused many times and, no, I could not have it altered. So I had to accept that. Vince eventually filled it out, but it was an awkward fit until he did.

Dick Toth coached Vincent during his first year (1991) on the varsity basketball team. Though he was always polite, and respectful of me and other parents, Toth was a fiery coach. He was a yell-in-your-face kind of a coach. He was a little like the old-school bad-boy college basketball coach Bobby Knight, but without the swearing and in-game chair tossing, just the passion and volume. This was the first coach that Vince had that was a 'yeller.'

In the rec leagues, coaches like this would have been a magnet for parent complaints, so they were rare. In AAU basketball, because parents paid a lot of money for their kids to play basketball, coaches tended to be tough and professional, but they never stepped over any comfort lines with the parents, who paid their bills. They wanted the best players on their team, and they wanted to be paid. But high school coaches were a little different. They worked for the school, not the parents. They could coach in whatever style worked for them, so long as they won. Coach Toth sure knew how to win. Mainland regularly won Districts and went deep into the state tournament under Coach Toth.

I was curious as to how Vince would respond to someone like Coach Toth. I knew from watching college games on TV that the loud in-your-face coaches were fairly common back in the 1990s. I figured Vince should experience this coaching style for himself. He adapted well to Coach Toth, who was truly an excellent coach all round. I'll confess that, as a parent, I felt pride watching how my son didn't flinch at all when Coach Toth yelled at him or the team. Vince was unflappable, kept his cool and responded well to whichever coach drew up in the huddle. The team also did well that year. Vince made a difference to every game he played in.

One of Coach Toth's assistant coaches, Charles Brinkerhoff, took over the reins during Vince's sophomore year (1992) and coached him through his senior year (1995). Fortunately, there were no politics within the Mainland boys' basketball coaching staff, and so this was a smooth transition of power. Coach Toth wished to retire from coaching, and he wanted Coach "Brink" to replace him. And that's what happened.

I cannot stress enough how important it is for a player's development to have a coach you trust, and who keeps his or her word. A coach who has your back in all situations.

I'm not sure that Vince would have developed his skills and ethics in such a healthy way in high school without the guidance of a series of excellent coaches. In the early 1990s it was significantly harder to transfer schools as a high school athlete too, so the coach–player dynamic was often determined simply by where you lived.

Back in the 1990s, like today, Mainland had a well established, competitive athletics program. We lived in an area called Tomoka Oaks in Ormond Beach, Florida. Vincent was zoned to attend school at Seabreeze High School. At that time, students could apply for an out-of-zone variance. If a student's parent worked at the desired school, the variance was usually approved. Since Vince's bonus dad was the music instructor and band director at Mainland, Vincent was good to go.

I've seen criticisms of parents who "coach shop" and move their kids around to find the best athletic program. Given how important coaching is, I see absolutely nothing wrong with this—except that moving can be hard on your kids. Again, I don't recommend specializing too early in sports. Parents also need to do their research.

Figuring out early on what are your expectations of a coach is key. Some general questions I would ask are as follows.

1) Is the coach trustworthy?
2) Do you respect the coach both on and off the court or field?
3) Does the coach truly know the sport, and are they considered elite by their peers?
4) Is the coach connected with college programs and scouts?
5) Are the athletes having fun?

And lastly, and perhaps most importantly,

6) Does my child respond well to this coach—is their skill set and level of play advancing in a direct and positive way?

There truly is a benefit to finding a coach that meets all of these expectations. Both Coach Toth and Coach Brink met them all.

My first interactions with Coach Brink were promising. Immediately, he and I bonded over our shared experience as educators. Like me, he was a teacher. He taught history at Mainland, and he excelled as an educator who was admired by his fellow teachers and students alike. One of the first things Coach Brink did after meeting me was bring me some SAT (Scholastic Aptitude Test) study books for Vince, which reassured me he knew education came first in my household.

I did have one incident with Coach Toth about Vince's priorities. For the most part Coach Toth and I were on the same page, but not on this occasion. One day, during Vince's first season with the Mainland Buccaneers (Bucs), Coach Toth scheduled a "two-a-day," which meant there were two full team practices that day—one after school and one in the evening. As a parent, I didn't love two-a-days, especially during the school year, but I understood the reasoning behind them, and usually had no issue with them.

When I picked Vince up from school at the end of the school day, the first thing he told me was the homework he was assigned, tests he needed to study for, and when everything was due. This was our after-school habit that let me know what was going on, and reminded him what he needed to do. Well Vince had an enormous list of school tasks that day. He had multiple tests to prepare for, in addition to many homework assignments from different classes. It was a much larger than usual workload. I realized there was no reasonable way Vince could attend that evening practice and be finished with the homework assignments before midnight. Vince also needed to get up at 6 a.m. for school, so he wouldn't be getting enough sleep if he went to the evening practice.

So I told Vince, "You're not going to be participating in the evening practice today." Vince was sad to hear this but accepted it. He was a little mopey doing his homework, but he got over it fast.

Student-athletes and parents must keep their eyes on the next prize and do what is necessary to academically qualify for that priceless college scholarship. Some parents would have given in and had their child take one for the team by attending the evening practice. I would not and did not. Some parents might have felt guilty they had to lay down the law and put their child at odds with the coach. I felt no guilt whatsoever. It is critical to clearly set boundaries early on so that potential parent–coach conflicts are avoided. I think that because I drew my boundaries clearly, and respectfully, early on, I never had another conflict with Coach Toth, and vice versa.

Coach Brink and I, meanwhile, never had even a single hint of conflict during the three years he coached Vince, beginning in his sophomore year. He also showed us his gratitude that Vince was so well prepared both on and off the court. Years later, Coach Brink wrote a memoir that included his experiences coaching Vince in high school. Coach Brinkerhoff assessed Vincent this way:

> When I first coached Vince, he was a very young player playing with much older and, at that time, more physically mature players on the Varsity team. Two of his older teammates would go on to play professional football. I had no real idea as to if, or how, this young 6'2" player would assume any real leadership role on this team. I would soon learn that Vince is a natural leader. His ability and desire to associate with all of his teammates and classmates of any race or background allowed Vince's natural persona to develop and he was seen by his peers as someone to look up to... literally and figuratively. As his athletic prowess grew, so did his leadership. His variety of talents, athletically, musically, and academically expanded his awareness and knowledge of how to interact and make an impact in a variety of situations.

Among other things, Coach Brink realized right away what an incredible work ethic Vince had. Vince was always the first to practice and the last to leave. Coach Brink also became a close family friend and adviser. For example, after Vincent began going to national tournaments and camps, Brink was so trusted by our family that he would pick Vince up at the airport when neither Harry nor I could do so.

  Coach Brink's coaching tenure was a success from the start. His first season, the team tallied a 21–7 record. He recently told me that when he had first taken over the head coaching job, he had tried too hard to be like Coach Toth. As mentioned, Coach Toth was a yeller, and Coach Brink, who is normally very mild mannered, tried to emulate his fiery ways. Coach Brink was very candid and told me that after his first season, when they went to the Final Four but lost, the school's Athletic Director, who was also the Mainland swim coach, told him, "You yell more than you coach." He said, "That stung".

  Coach Brink took this comment to heart and realized he needed to alter his approach with the team. He needed to tone it down: yell less and coach more. By his own admission, Brink himself had never been an elite athlete, even in high school, so he didn't have many personal coach mentors to draw upon. He regarded Coach Toth as his top mentor, so it's not surprising he had mistakenly tried to imitate his coaching style.

  Coach Brink started to study the game of basketball more himself. He read University of North Carolina (UNC) Coach Dean Smith's book about basketball "Xs and Os" called, *Basketball: Multiple Offense and Defense.* If you don't know what "Xs and Os" are, they are how a basketball coach (or any coach) represents their players on a dry erase board when they draw up plays during practice or the in-game huddle. Some coaches operate more on instinct, some are pure technicians who depend on "Xs and Os" charts. The best coaches are probably a mix of the two. Coach Brink swore that Dean Smith's *Basketball Multiple Offense and Defense* was the only book you needed to read to get your team to win the state championship back in the 1990s.

In addition to becoming more of a tactical coach, Coach Brink also yelled less at the boys and listened more. He used the input of the players, like Vince, to help him design plays. The team responded, and their talents grew and took them far. Coach Brink would go on to boast a final overall 176–45 win–loss record as head coach at Mainland, including winning three Florida State Basketball Championships, and four Final Four appearances. Whatever Coach Brink paid for that Dean Smith book, it was clearly a bargain.

In 1994, Vince and the Mainland High School boys' basketball team found themselves in their first Final Four of the Florida State Basketball Championships. This was Vincent's junior year, and the basketball team held a hard-earned 30–1 record going into the Final Four. Imagine your team is good enough to go 30–1 during both the regular season and deep into the playoffs—that's got to be a real confidence builder. But sometimes athletes get a bit too cocky.

Although I had always tried to prevent Vince from falling into that trap, I'm pretty sure he and his teammates thought they were a shoo-in to win the State Championship that year. They may indeed have been a little too cocky; so much so, that the morning before their state semifinal game, more than half of the boys on the team shaved their heads in the "spirit of unity," or some such thing. The head-shaving took place in one of the boys' shared hotel rooms. I knew nothing about this before the game. I just saw the boys come out of the locker room tunnel into their pre-game huddle, most of them as bald as the next. That was a lot of head shine. To say that I was perplexed upon witnessing the boys after this anti-follicular event would be an understatement. But I went with it; I was pretty worked up for the game myself.

Mainland High School was favored to win the semifinal against Boyd Anderson High School, from Lauderdale Lakes, Florida. They had a record of 28–5. The semifinal game did not go well for the Mainland Bucs. The Boyd Anderson Cobras got off to a hot start, and the Mainland boys were playing catch-up the entire game. The Bucs were usually the ones to get the early lead, so they were stunned at this turn of events. Maybe they didn't recognize each other with their newly shaved heads. I'm not sure. I do know that Vince had a solid game, but some of his teammates struggled. The Buccaneers experienced the agony of defeat, losing 61–66 to the Cobras. The Boyd Anderson boys would go on to win the State Championship game, too. This Final Four was clearly the biggest game that anyone on the Bucs team had ever played. To have it end in such a heart-breaking way was tough. Going home bald on the team bus probably didn't improve anybody's spirits either.

Years after the game, one of the team's starters, Joe Giddens, explained to me their pre-game bonding ritual, which in retrospect had probably been a mistake because it robbed them of their "mojo". Joe, one of Vince's closest friends to this day, still felt badly about the event decades later.

Joe was a two-sport varsity athlete who played both basketball and football. He was good enough to play both sports in college too—at Bethune-Cookman. He even went on to play pro football in the Canadian League with the Toronto Argonauts. Joe is now the current Mainland boys' basketball head coach, and he's done an amazing job in the role.

Although none of the parents or coaches knew about the head shaving in advance, we all sure heard about it afterwards. Though Coach Brink was as surprised as the rest of us about the boys' actions, he was the one who got scolded. The boys had left an absolute mess behind in the LaQuinta Hotel room where the group head shaving had taken place. Our local school board, who had to pay for the damages, were informed by the LaQuinta managers that the room "looked like a crime scene." I wasn't hard on Vince at all about the hotel room incident, even though it was a dumb idea. I didn't need to punish Vince; he was quite hard on himself about losing the game. Even though the team had made it all the way to the semifinals, he felt like he had failed—that he personally had let the team, the school, his family, and the community down. At that moment, it was far more important for me to show my support for Vince and the rest of the team. Alongside this, I also knew that Vince had learned a prime life lesson about over-confidence.

Coach Brink was also deeply affected by the loss, even though just getting to the Final Four had still been an impressive accomplishment. He questioned whether he had what it took to win the state title. Coach Brink told me, years later, that after the loss to Boyd Anderson he had developed a kind of simple mantra (though he didn't call it that) to "Focus. Be more present." In my eyes, Coach Brink was already a thoughtful, focused man, so this intrigued me.

Immediately after the loss, Vincent became obsessed with getting back to the State Championship game and winning it in his senior year. This obsession became a bit concerning to me. Vincent was constantly talking about getting back. Coach Brink recently told me that there had even been a *Sports Illustrated* article written around this time where Vince was quoted saying, "we intend to come back next year, and we intend to win."

After the loss to Boyd Anderson in March, all the boys on the team still had to go to a seventh-period study hall class every school day until the end of the year. These team study halls are common in high school, and I fully approve because they help make sure that homework gets done. Now, in this team study hall, the boys took responsibility for the loss and started to develop the resolve they would need to win the title the following year. The loss really inspired Vince to become more of a leader. In his junior year, he averaged 27 points a game. He scored a similar amount in the team's semifinal loss to Boyd Anderson. But now Vince realized he needed to trust his teammates more and put them in better positions to win. As I said, Vince was the first to practice and the last to leave. He also got his teammates to buy in and practice more, and harder too. He organized summer practices and pushed his teammates by challenging them to win the title.

Even before the school year began, the Bucs played some summer tournaments at Florida State, the University of Florida, and other venues. The team also played in the prestigious Beach Ball Classic in Myrtle Beach, South Carolina. In these tournaments, the boys would play seven to nine games with other elite teams from the southeast of the United States. Joe Giddens recalls one game against a team from Thomasville, Georgia. Vince had hurt his right wrist to the point that he couldn't shoot with that hand, but he still insisted upon playing. Because he couldn't use his right hand, he shot with his left hand the entire game and managed to make six 3-point shots. He was on a mission.

I knew that the 1994–95 Mainland Buccaneer Basketball Team would be stellar. Vince's teammates were T. T. Toliver, Joe Giddens, O. C. Burks, Desmond Long, Tres Walton, Duran Williams, Han Ripley, Al Sermon, Kaylo Hannah, Donnie Gray, and Ryan Hill. They had the goods. It was just a matter of pulling it together. More easily said than done—after all, these were still just children. But somehow Vincent (the captain of the team), head coach Charles Brinkerhoff, and assistant coaches Derrick Henry, Sean Beckton, Clifford Reed, and the late Alvin Hawthorne all bought in.

During Vince's senior year, in early 1995, the team finished the regular season with a 34–2 record. Back to the State Championship game they went. This time, the team had played in major basketball tournaments in and outside Florida and had been to the Final Four already. They had experience. They were ready.

According to Coach Brink, Joe, and my son, the hardest game they played that entire year was not the actual championship game but the semifinal game. Their opponent in that game was a tough Miami Senior High School team. The Miami team included future NBA player Udonis Haslem (later with the Miami Heat), who was to become famous for his toughness and longevity in the NBA. The team was coached by Frank Martin, who at time of writing is the men's basketball head coach at the University of Massachusetts, after being a successful head coach at Kansas State and the University of South Carolina. In the four years he was head coach at Miami Senior High School, Coach Martin would go on to win three future Florida State Championships—but not in 1995. Even though the Miami High Stingrays had an obvious height advantage over the Mainland Bucs team, it didn't matter. Vince and his team were locked in.

The 1995 State Championship Final Four was held at the Tallahassee Leon County Civic Center, located in the middle of the Florida Panhandle. This was the last time the Final Four would be held in Tallahassee; afterwards, the Final Four moved to Lakeland, Florida, where it remains today. Tallahassee was about a five-hour drive from Mainland High School. That didn't matter. The Buccaneers were well represented. Many fans made the drive. Some rode on chartered school buses—over 500 Mainland fans went to the game this way.

Even though I believed one hundred percent in my son and his team, I was a little nervous about this game. Vincent had become so obsessed with winning the title, I was genuinely worried what would happen if the team lost again. I wanted to show my complete support, so I stood in the crowded Mainland fan section, with my sisters, my parents, and many friends, holding up a sign I'd made that read, "Unfinished Business" in large, bold letters. I was relieved when the boys came out of the tunnel with their hair styles intact.

Miami's game plan was clearly to rattle Vince. The Miami boys double-teamed him, bumped him, or got into his face whenever they could. Vince didn't care; he was unflappable and brought everything he had to the game. He was playing so aggressively that he got into a little bit of foul trouble, but it didn't matter—every boy on the Bucs played to the maximum of his ability. The Bucs squeaked by to win the game

70–67, despite Vincent sitting out more than his teammates were accustomed to him doing.

There would be no repeat of foul trouble in the championship game against Fort Lauderdale Dillard. The Bucs took care of business, winning handily by a score of 62–45. These young men were on a mission, and the mission was accomplished. The 1995 Florida's state boys' basketball champions were the Mainland High School Buccaneers! It had been 56 years since Mainland High School had last won a state basketball championship (1939).

After Vince graduated, Coach Brink went on to win the Florida State Championship twice more, in 1996 and 1998. He retired with a fantastic win–loss record of 176–45.

One of Coach Brink's stories about Vince summed up how magical their time together was:

> After practice one day, the guys were just having fun and challenging each other to jump as high as they could and leave a handprint on the backboard. After everyone had a chance at this feat, it was Vince's turn. Vince looked at his teammates and said, "watch this." He took two or three long strides toward the backboard, then jumped up, and from a slight distance it looked as if Vince had touched the rubber casing at the top of the backboard. As if that weren't enough, Vince insisted that he had actually touched the *top* of the backboard. While there was no way to prove he had touched the top, it was an amazing feat, nonetheless. After the basketball season was over, a cleaning crew took down the backboard for maintenance. As the backboard was pulled down to the floor, Vince and I happened to be walking in the gym. As I walked by the lowered backboard, before the crew began to work on it, I noticed how dusty the top of the backboard was… except for the swiped fingerprints that ONLY could have been made by Vince that afternoon a few months earlier. Vince just walked over, took a look at the prints, and said, "See, I told you so."

Soon after the state championship celebrations, parade, and presentation of rings and jackets were over, the basketball awards and honors came rolling in for Vince. He was selected as a McDonald's All-America, Parade All-America, and USA Today All-America player; Florida's Mr. Basketball

(1994-95); and Gatorade Player of the Year (Regional 1995). He became a finalist for the James Naismith High School Player-of-the-Year; and he was selected to the USA Junior National Select Basketball Team and as the McDonald's All-America Slam Dunk Champion.

    By the time the Bucs won the Florida State Championship, Vince was being pursued by 77 NCAA basketball programs, including most elite programs across the United States. Vincent finished his high school basketball play with 2299 points, 1042 rebounds, 356 assists, and 178 steals. Yeah, so maybe I still didn't see him becoming a professional athlete one day, but I sure knew he would soon be playing college basketball somewhere.

6

College Recruitment Chaos

Vincent Carter got his first letter of interest to play college basketball when he was only twelve. My initial thought was, "They've got to be joking. He's only twelve years old!" I didn't put much stock in this letter from the University of Indiana, because it was mind-boggling that such a prestigious college basketball team, coached by the great Bobby Knight, would be seriously interested in a twelve-year-old. I soon learned, however, that this had become the trend for college athletic programs—get to the athlete early and often. Over the next several years, the number of recruitment letters grew exponentially.

Being recruited by even one college or university, no matter how large or small, or what division, is exciting. But if there is not a plan in place to handle the emails, texts, "snail-mail," visits and other pressures, this exciting time can turn into a nightmare. Believe me, I learned the hard way.

By the time Vince made his decision during the spring of his senior year in high school, 77 colleges or universities had expressed an interest in having him attend their institution of higher learning. The big names in college basketball were all represented: Duke, University of North Carolina (UNC), Kentucky, and Kansas, as well as the standout programs in Florida, including the University of Florida and Florida State. The last of the 77 scholarship offers even came in the form of a music scholarship, offered by none other than my alma mater, Bethune-Cookman University.

With just about every elite NCAA basketball program interested in Vince, perhaps you're wondering how it was even possible that I still wasn't sure he'd play in the NBA someday. In retrospect, it seemed everyone around us, back then, thought he was destined to go pro, including some very famous college coaches. But not me. Remember Vince's uncle Oliver Lee, who was one of the top high school players in Florida?

I recently learned that top area coaches and local hardcore basketball fans still generally regard Vince and Oliver Lee as the two best basketball players ever from Volusia County. Like Vince, Oliver also led his team, the DeLand Bulldogs, to the State Championship game, in 1977. That's how good Oliver was. DeLand lost that game, but it was still very impressive they made it that far. Also remember that after four years playing basketball at Marquette, including a standout senior season, Oliver Lee was drafted by the Chicago Bulls. But then he was unceremoniously cut during his rookie season. That was the NBA reality that I personally witnessed—it was hard to go pro, even for the most elite of high school athletes.

Fifteen or so years later, after Vince's team won the Florida State Championship, I still remembered his uncle's brief NBA career. It served as my reality check about my own son's prospects. This was healthy for me. No matter how good Vince was, I always had my reasons to keep my expectations in check. I never told Vince about this; I would never do anything to undermine his confidence. But I always made sure my son had a plan B, though Vince was reluctant to even think of an alternative.

We all knew for sure that Vince was going to college, which had always been the plan A, regardless of whether he played sports or not. Managing his college recruitment process, however, resembled a full-time job. The volume of mail and phone calls I received, particularly in his senior year, was often overwhelming. On slow days, Vince would receive a letter or two. On busy days, he received a literal pile of mail. One of the NCAA recruitment rules back then was that college coaches couldn't send prospects news clippings about their program or player successes. So all the letters received were original letters, addressed to either Vince, his high school head coach, Charles Brinkerhoff, or sometimes even Harry and me, the parents. The letter in which the late great Coach Dean Smith introduced himself to Vince is shown in the first illustration section of this book. My favorite part of the letter was this paragraph:

> Coach Guthridge [UNC Assistant Coach] indicated that your parents are school teachers. This is impressive to me and to Coach Phil Ford, since we grew up in homes where our mothers and fathers were teachers. Even though you deserve credit being a tremendous young man and an outstanding student-athlete, I know you give credit to your parents as well.

By now you know how important education is to me and my family, and how much we revere great teachers. This was a smart move by Coach Smith. I knew that by the time he wrote to Vince Coach Smith had written hundreds of prospect letters, but his correspondence always seemed personal, without being pushy. It's an art form. I learned that some college coaches left the letter writing to their assistant coaches and saved their energies for phone calls or in-person visits. Some programs sent out form letters, which were easy to spot. But the most famous and elite coaches, like Dean Smith and Duke's head coach, Mike Krzyzewski (aka "Coach K"), wrote us many handwritten letters. They made sure you knew how much they cared.

Coach Dean Smith even had his own note card stationery that had different dimensions from the stationery that his assistant coaches used. Coach Smith's handwritten notes always came in a diminutive envelope, made from quality stock paper, which from the outside made a letter from him look more like a wedding invite than something from a coach. Without even opening the letter, you knew Coach Smith cared about you.

I'm not sure how it works nowadays with texting, email, and social media. Regardless, you can tell a college program is serious about your prospects if the head coach is communicating directly with you. The illustration section also shows a handwritten note from Coach K. Although it was brief, one could see that he did his homework and was on top of what was happening in Vince's world.

Because I thought Vince might want to reminisce about his college recruitment correspondence some day, I kept the letters from all 77 college programs that pursued him to be a student-athlete. Part of my garage, in fact, serves as a makeshift shrine to Vincent's recruitment process, as I have at least a half dozen large bins stacked full of letters he received from every college program that wanted to sign him. Mainland High School is known for having stellar athletes in various sports, but I learned no one had been recruited at the level of Vincent Carter. I still have the boxes in my garage to prove it.

Another critical part of the college recruitment process is making visits to colleges. When Vincent visited Florida State, his host was one of his favorite college players, Charlie Ward. As already mentioned, Charlie was a stellar two-sport athlete: a football quarterback and a basketball point guard for the Seminoles, and he was the 1992 Heisman Trophy winner. I remember fearing that once Vince returned from his visit in Tallahassee with Charlie, the two-sport talk would start again. Fortunately, Vince stayed focused on basketball.

Coach Brink was also instrumental in the final period of Vince's college recruitment process. Often Vince's recruitment mail was sent directly to him, or both to him and to our home. Coach Brink was very proactive in the process, though never pushy or overbearing. He wanted Vince to decide what was best for him. Some of the earliest advice Coach Brink gave me was to encourage me to sign Vince up for some of those elite national basketball camps, so he could get more national exposure among college coaches and scouts. Coach Brink based his recommendations for camps on which ones regularly made the national and regional sports news, and on flyers that were sent to him from invitation-only camps. There was of course no Google at that time, so this is how the reputations of the best camps were spread—by mail, sports news, and word-of-mouth.

Coach Brink wanted Vince to attend the elite camps not just to achieve national exposure but to understand how good he was. Vince already knew he was a big fish in a small pond. Brink wanted him to see he was a big fish in the ocean. Vince did meet other 'big fish' at the camps: Kobe Bryant, Antwan Jamison, Kevin Garnett, and many more. Coach Brink has a great story about Kevin Garnett and Vince:

> Vince and I traveled to Chicago for the NIKE High School All-American Camp the summer before his senior year. While there, we and the other NIKE All-American players and coaches were being transported in a school bus to a practice facility. Sitting in the back of the bus, Vince introduced me to his new friend, Kevin Garnett. When Kevin heard my name, he said, "Coach Break-You-Off? (That's the best name ever for a coach!) Hey Coach, what if I come down to Daytona and play with you and Vince this year?" Sarcastically I said, "Sure, come on down," without any serious thought to the matter. Kevin persisted, "No, Coach… for REAL!" I continued laughing and playing the conversation down, being the young, naïve coach that I was. Shortly after camp, the newspapers reported that Kevin Garnett had indeed transferred from his high school in South Carolina to Farragut High School in Chicago. It turns out that Kevin actually was looking to transfer high schools. If I had been a little wiser to

the ways of the coaching world I had recently entered, Kevin Garnett might have been a teammate of Vince Carter in high school.

This happened back in 1994, and it would not be the last time that Kevin Garnett would exuberantly congratulate Vince on his awe-inspiring dunks. Little did they know, the 2000 Olympics would be a backdrop for a dunk that would be talked about for generations to come. More on that later.

Coach Brinkerhoff is a very humble man, but he took every opportunity to pick the brains of the great coaches who were vying for Vince. This afforded Coach Brink a reason to step into many of their inner circles. It's rare that a high school coach gets the opportunity to talk basketball with coaches like Dean Smith, Roy Williams, and Mike Krzyzewski. But Coach Brink did. He made new friends and learned many tips that he later used with his own high school teams.

Coach Smith, Coach Krzyzewski, and other top coaches visited Mainland High School to watch Vince play in person and to meet our family. Back in the 1990s, the Mainland High School gym was nothing to brag about. It was cramped, had terrible acoustics, and—most significantly for Florida—there was no air conditioning. Even though high school basketball is a "winter" sport, this means something different in Florida. Rarely did the Daytona Beach temperature go much below 70° F, and with so many people in the gym the collective body heat could raise the temperature to an uncomfortable level, particularly for visiting head coaches wearing full suits with ties.

Amidst all the hype surrounding the college recruitment, Vince just wanted to go to college. He knew that a college degree was expected of him. He also knew that students, even gifted athletes, can't just *want* to go to college; they must *prepare* to go to college. That means achieving the highest score they can on standardized tests, maintaining a respectable grade point average with classwork, engaging in community service and being well rounded.

Even for a diligent student like Vince, taking the SAT (Scholastic Aptitude Test), ACT (American College Testing) and other tests could be daunting. Individuals are different in their learning and test-taking styles. In preparation for college entry, Vincent took the SAT and ACT tests several times. Each session, he would eat a healthy breakfast and listen to music to calm himself prior to taking his seat for the exams. Each time, he would achieve a higher score, which was the plan. There was no shame in taking the tests multiple times; it's how you learn.

Now it's true that some colleges do bend the rules, or admission standards, for athletes, meaning that if you're a great athlete, your SAT scores and the like don't necessarily have to be so great. Everyone knows this happens, even at some of the NCAA powerhouse colleges. But I raised Vince with the idea he could compete with anyone in the gym or in the classroom. I made him want to get a high SAT score, not because he needed it for admission, but to prove to himself he would fit in at the most academically elite schools. This also reassured me that he would do well in college, and that he had the smarts for any program that wanted him, including vaunted institutions like UNC and Duke. I can recall scheduling Vincent's final SAT attempt for a sitting in Detroit, Michigan. It was the last opportunity for him to take the test prior to him entering college in the fall of 1995. Vincent had been invited to play in the Magic Johnson Roundball Classic in Detroit. This presented a conflict with his last chance to get his SAT test score even higher. But we made it work. We arrived in Detroit a day early. The organizers of the basketball event assisted us in navigating our way to the testing site and hotel. Parents and guardians should, in my view, utilize all the resources and assistance that may be available, especially on the road. Exhaust every option to achieve the goal.

I remember trying to gather as much intelligence on potential college coaches and programs as I could, from any source I could. At one of Vince's senior year tournaments—the Beachball Classic in Myrtle Beach, South Carolina—I remember asking Antawn Jamison, who was a high school senior playing for another team, why he committed to UNC. Vince had narrowed his college choices down to seven schools by then, including UNC, so any bit of information about the school helped. To this day, Antawn remembers me approaching him and asking him whether Dean Smith was really like he was on TV—if he was really that sincere and kind-hearted. Vince and I saw interviews with Coach Smith where he seemed more approachable and less volatile than many of his elite peers. In temperament, Coach Smith seemed more like Coach Brink than, say, Bobby Knight. Antawn reassured me Dean Smith was exactly as advertised, and that he had chosen UNC for a variety of reasons including the coaches, academics, and quality of student life.

Even after all the letters, college visits, coach visits, standardized tests, and my intelligence gathering, Vincent still had a big decision to make, and it was his to make; I could only offer my best guidance and pray. So, how does one manage to eliminate 76 colleges to arrive at THE ONE? You do it methodically. There must be a plan. I developed a handwritten spreadsheet to organize any data or notes I had on college programs and coaches. This was used to track the pros and cons of each college/university. With 77 choices, this list had to be extremely detailed. We even charted how the basketball staff would help the players celebrate holidays such as Thanksgiving and Christmas, when they often spend more time with the team than their families. This is usually when freshmen feel most homesick, as they miss their families and holiday traditions.

It is important to prepare thoroughly for the time when your student-athlete will leave home for college. Before they even commit to a college, campus visits will help them gauge their comfort level with other student-athletes and the surroundings while on campus. In the 1990s, five official visits to the prospect schools were permitted. A student-athlete could also make unofficial visits as long as there was no interaction with the coaching staff or the team—something that I'd recommend.

When everyone knows that a top recruit is coming to campus on an official visit, the dog-and-pony show is in full effect, meaning they go to great efforts to make things appear like a student paradise (which it may or may not be). It's advisable for the student-athlete and their parents to ask as many and as varied questions as they feel they need to, as this will put them at ease concerning the day-to-day life on the campus, and when the student-athlete travels.

I found that it is smart, sooner rather than later, to set up some recruiting rules for your home, governing when coaches can call or visit the house. Unfortunately, I got to that "Oh hell, no!" place, where I felt the rules had already been violated before they were even put in place. I had no guidebook to help Vincent through this process.

Believe me, boundaries were necessary. Coaches are by nature competitive people who seek out any advantage they can to get to a recruit. It's your job as a parent to make sure the process runs smoothly and respectfully, and that your child is never overwhelmed or coerced.

During what is called the "live period," coaching staff are permitted by NCAA rules to contact recruits. That's wonderful, but as a parent you have to be prepared to say: "You can't call my home after 10 p.m. Eastern Time, to speak with my son!" Any parents reading this will know how difficult it is to make sure that a sleep-deprived teenager is up at 6:00 a.m. To stop those midnight calls from the West Coast coaches, one of the house rules was: *no calls after 10:00 p.m.* It didn't matter whether the calls were coming from the East, the West or the moon!

The recruitment process was so overwhelming at times that I encouraged Vince to make his decision in the early spring of 1995, so that he could relax and enjoy the rest of his senior year without pressure or interruptions. I wanted him to focus on his friends and doing the fun and silly stuff that seniors do as their high school careers wind down.

Meanwhile, after attending elite camps and AAU tournaments, and making the State Championship game, Vincent became a household name amongst those around the country that followed high school basketball. So much so that, during the spring break of his senior year, he received the prestigious invitation to play in the 1995 International Basketball Federation (FIBA) Men's Junior World Basketball Tournament as a member of Team USA.

The United States junior team, which also included future NBA star Stephon Marbury, was ranked number 7 in the world, because even though they were loaded with talent, the team was hastily constructed and lacked playing time together, unlike most of the other national teams. The tournament, which took place in Greece, was an exciting time for Vince, even if the team didn't quite gel. They finished seventh in the tournament, upset by four other teams, including the host team Greece, who won the Gold—but in accordance with their ranking, so it was still a respectable result.

After the FIBA tournament, Vince returned home and, in a jam-packed Mainland High School gym, made his final college decision. This announcement was a big deal at his school. Everyone at Mainland High had got tuned in to the hype around his recruitment process—students, teachers, custodians, the principal, and, of course, the basketball team and coaching staff. Mathematics teachers, including Vincent's trigonometry teacher Mrs. Suzanne Gibson, even used the regularity of receiving his recruitment letters at the school to teach algorithms and statistics!

Mainland's principal, Tim Huth, excused students from their seventh-period classes to come to the gym to hear the announcement. There were more media folks in the gym than I had ever witnessed. I am sure that 76 schools were waiting to hear as well (the basketball staff at the school Vince had chosen were of course already aware that they had got the prize!)

In front of the massive crowd, Vincent stood up and placed the cap of the University of North Carolina at Chapel Hill on his head. The crowd went crazy! Sports writers and media photographers rushed closer to get their photos of Vince with his UNC cap, then scampered out of the door to get their stories in the can.

For the parents and the athlete, the moment of making the school choice announcement brings a feeling of great relief. There were a couple of months during which different media outlets were wanting to know the process that had led Vincent to his decision. Some wanted to know why he hadn't chosen Duke (Mike Krzyzewski), Florida (Lon Kruger), Florida State (Pat Kennedy), Kentucky (Rick Pitino), or Kansas (Roy Williams). It had been well publicized that, along with UNC, these schools made the final six. But ultimately the choice came down to Vince and what he wanted. Now that the decision was announced, all I wanted was for Vincent to exhale and enjoy the rest of his high school senior year. Then it would be time for him to say, "Chapel Hill, here I come!"

The Making of Vince Carter

7

The Carolina Way

It's difficult to describe just how much hype surrounded Vince going to the University of North Carolina at Chapel Hill. Although he'd been ranked nationally as a player for a few years and his tournament wins received media coverage, Vince's college commitment announcement was the first time he became a true national story. The local hype Vince encountered at Mainland High School paled into insignificance by comparison. Vince's choice of UNC was a big deal not only in our local community but also across Florida, where some fans felt a little betrayed that Vince had selected an out-of-state school over Florida State University and the University of Florida, two schools that made his final list. Fortunately, social media didn't exist yet, so we didn't have to see or hear too much about their disappointment.

Nationally, college basketball reporters and fans were wondering whether UNC was possibly forming another Dean Smith college super team. Previous Tar Heel teams under their head coach Dean Smith had twice won the National Championship and were nearly a fixture in the Sweet Sixteen, Elite Eight, and Final Four rounds of the NCAA

Tournament. When Vince committed to UNC, the team was already stacked with elite talent, including forwards Jerry Stackhouse and Rasheed Wallace, who would both go on to become NBA All-Stars. That UNC squad was so good that it made the Final Four in the NCAA Tournament the year before Vince arrived. In fact, when Vince committed to UNC, he wasn't sure if he'd even start during his freshman year. This was not only because the 1995–96 Tar Heel squad was so deep, but also because Dean Smith famously did not start freshmen. To this day, part of Dean Smith's legacy is that he didn't start the great Michael Jordan at first, as a freshman, during the 1981–82 season. That's right: MJ started his UNC career on the bench! It wasn't until November 28th, 1981, in their game against Kansas, that Coach Smith thought MJ was ready for a starting role. That's some coaching resolve. But, hey, the Tar Heels won the Atlantic Coast Conference (ACC) Tournament and Championship that same season, so clearly Coach Smith knew what he was doing.

Even if he couldn't count on starting, Vince was so ready to be a Tar Heel. He couldn't wait to shine on their court. He appreciated his budding relationships with Dean Smith and the assistant coaches, as well as the chemistry he had already developed with future teammates, like Antawn Jamison.

Vince was so eager that I was a little worried about how he'd fare academically. I constantly reminded Vince that he was a student-athlete: student first, athlete second. My expectations for him involved three basic things: to earn a college degree, to play basketball to the best of his ability, and to stay out of trouble. Vince adhered to all three. In retrospect, I had it easier than some sports parents, but I still imposed some rules when he started college.

Vince is my eldest child. Therefore, he was the first child in the household to attend college. As an educator, I believed that it made a lot of sense for a college freshman to get through that first year before having a vehicle on campus.

There are so many adjustments that freshmen must make, and I wanted to keep it simple. In most cases freshmen have more freedom than they are accustomed to. It is easy for a young student to get off-course, so it's important to reduce the temptations. A vehicle is nice, but it can easily lead to trouble.

Vince knew that one of our main house rules was "no grades, no play." I hoped that after so many years of adhering to this it would be engrained in him. Thankfully, there was never a problem with Vince and this rule while he was in college. The NCAA has academic requirements in place as well. Vince knew he was there first and foremost for an education, even if everyone else assumed he was there primarily to play ball. He and I both knew that if for any reason basketball failed him he would have a college degree that would assist him in finding a quality career.

As a parent, the goal for me was for my eldest child to earn a college degree which would be enable him to attain a well paid job and career. Making it to the NBA was Vince's dream, and plan A, of course. Who could blame him? He'd worked so hard on his game to be the best he could be. I knew that he had a better chance than most. But the overall odds were still stark.

According to recent NCAA statistics, only 3.5% of high school boys and 4.1% of high school girls play collegiate basketball after high school. The chances of making the NBA are frightfully small—about 3 in 10,000 boys who play high school basketball will eventually be drafted into the NBA—only 0.03%! The chances of a player on an NCAA men's basketball team making the NBA are considerably better, at 1.2%, but those are still a fool's odds, no matter how gifted a player is. Plus, many of those who are drafted won't have long NBA careers—the average career in NBA lasts just 4.5 years. Again, I remembered Oliver Lee's short tenure with the Chicago Bulls. But I also knew that Vince still had a better chance than most, and learning some basketball wisdom from the great Dean Smith and the UNC basketball brain trust was only going to help.

The first time Vince and I visited the University of North Carolina at Chapel Hill was during the winter school break of Vince's senior year, right after he and his Mainland High School basketball team attended the Beach Ball Classic tournament in Myrtle Beach, South Carolina. As there was no GPS (satnav) at that time, Coach Smith wanted to make sure we knew how to get there, so around Christmas time in 1994 he sent me a personal note that included a map of the Carolinas cut out from an atlas, with a highlighted path from Myrtle Beach to Chapel Hill. After that was a separate map clipping of the greater Raleigh, NC, area, with the path to UNC's campus highlighted, followed by a map of the campus with an arrow pointing to the Athletic Department building where his office was located. Finally, there was a little scrap of paper with Coach Smith's handwritten instructions explaining where to park. As a detail-oriented person myself, I appreciated Coach Smith's initiative. Unsurprisingly, we had no problem finding the campus and parking in the appropriate place. Coach Smith made sure of that.

Even in winter time, with the leaves off the trees and the weather colder, Chapel Hill was beautiful. I remember driving down the broad tree-lined streets wondering, "Could this be the place that Vince selects?" When I saw the cozy shops and boutiques on Franklin Street, I liked it even more, as I like to shop! But I tried to remain neutral, of course. At that moment, Vince was seriously interested in more than half a dozen schools, and I wasn't sure where UNC stood in his pecking order.

Several of Vince's former high school friends recently told me that they were convinced he was going to choose Florida State. That made sense because FSU was the college football team Vince rooted for and admired the most. Plus, he had that FSU campus visit with one of his idols in Charlie

Ward. So when we visited UNC I didn't invest in it too much, beyond noticing the town was lovely. After Vince declared UNC was his choice, I looked forward to spending a lot of time in Chapel Hill.

On the first drive directly from Ormond Beach, FL, to Chapel Hill, NC, in the summer of 1995, the conversations were all over the place. Vince's bonus dad was driving; I was the front passenger-seat co-pilot, while Vince had the entire back seat to himself. I am sure that Vince, being 6'6" tall, appreciated that space. One of the topics of discussion was the importance of Vince committing to earn his bachelor's degree.

Most members of our family hold a bachelor's degree, while some have master's degrees, and a few have earned or received honorary doctoral degrees. In my mind, it was imperative that Vince understood the importance of Black Americans garnering as much education as possible. During that drive to UNC, I felt the need to get his commitment to education in writing. In the car I didn't have any paper, so I took a napkin and wrote out a simple contract. The agreement was between Vince and me. He signed the agreement, promising that if he left UNC early he would return to finish the requirements for his bachelor's degree. I know this was just a napkin scribble that held no real legal value, but it made me feel better. Vince always kept his word.

Vince's first declared major was Communications. I felt he had made a good choice there, because he was articulate, poised, and did not have a problem with subject-verb agreement. He also possessed a special charisma which makes him a natural in front of the camera. Then, without consulting me, Vince changed his major to African American Studies. Apparently, several of the guys on the basketball team decided to collectively change majors. Once I was made aware of Vince's switch in majors, it did not sit well with me because I didn't feel that it was his decision. It seemed more like he was just going along with the group.

At that time, I also wasn't sure what careers this degree led to, unlike studying Communications. I had to let him, as a young adult, plot his own course, so I did—though the last time he and his teammates made a big group decision, they all ended up losing the big game, and bald! But I had to trust that this decision would work out better. It was sometimes hard letting go as a parent.

I had a similar experience of having to let go with regard to Vincent's name. Sometimes already in this book I have referred to Vince Carter by his birth name, Vincent, as well as by its shortened form, Vince. Well, I pretty much exclusively called him Vincent for his entire childhood and teen years. During Vincent's high school years, however, after his celebrity exploded, everyone started calling him Vince, including coaches, teachers and reporters. Some even shortened his name to "VC". This trend did not go down easily with me or my family. In fact, there are a few family members who still call him Vincent to this day. I will admit that I, too, was a holdout until Vincent entered the NBA, when I felt odd calling him Vincent because no one else on the team, or in the media, or anywhere else was. Letting go of "Vincent" as his name was hard for me. But many other parents will have had a similar experience, and as a parent you need to know when to adapt your ways.

Meanwhile, at UNC, I witnessed my son adapting to new ways of playing basketball. He had to, if he wanted to play for Coach Dean Smith, one of the best college basketball coaches in history. Coach Dean Smith's UNC teams won two National Championships and appeared in eleven Final Fours. He was so revered that he was inducted into the Basketball Hall of Fame in 1983, years even before Vince played for his team. Coach Smith's famed book on basketball strategy, *Basketball: Multiple Offense and Defense*—that same book that helped Coach Brink and Vince's team win the Florida High School Championship—is still the top-selling technical basketball book of all time. Coach Brink and Vince can testify that its advice works.

Sadly, Coach Smith passed away in 2015, but his legacy lives on through many coaches and players alike who practice the "Carolina Way" of playing basketball. The Carolina Way is a particularly team-oriented and technical way of playing basketball. Many NCAA programs rely on raw talent first and foremost. The success of their teams is thus mostly dependent upon the skills of whom they recruit. The Carolina Way relies instead on building up the basketball IQ, teamwork skills, and trust of every player in the program. The UNC program is not just a vehicle for the star players to drive.

There were times that the way Vince played basketball didn't jive with the Carolina Way. Vince is a colorful, demonstrative basketball player. More than one person has called him a "show-off" in his life, including me! In his home state, one of his nicknames was "Florida Flash". However, the Carolina Way is that each player has a role; you play your role and don't veer away from that. Yet Vince was coming out of a high school basketball program where he was Mr. Everything. His role was to do whatever he could humanly do to help the team win the game. There were times when what he did didn't look very human at all. This was sometimes an issue when he started at UNC.

I can recall Vince's first Midnight Madness event in the Dean Dome at UNC. Midnight Madness was the semi-official late-night event that kicked off the Tar Heel basketball season, where new and returning players are introduced, and then adulated by diehard UNC fans on their homecourt. Vince's first Madness event was in October 1995, when he was a freshman. During the rehearsal of the introductions, players were to walk to center-court and wave to the crowd. Vince walked to center-court, and instead of waving to the crowd he offered a gentleman's bow. The crowd went nuts! Apparently, this was too flashy for Coach Smith. Vince stood out from the other players, which was not the Carolina Way.

That bow was written about more than I could understand. I didn't get the fuss—it was just a bow! Student-athletes conducting themselves within the parameters of the athletic program is one thing, but those parameters can be too restrictive. My advice is for athletes to play by the rules, but also to understand when the rules are a bit irrational. Never allow the coaching staff to rob your student-athletes of their individuality.

Vince became life-long friends with his teammates, especially Antawn Jamison and Ademola Okulaja. Ademola and Antawn became freshman student-athletes at UNC in 1995. The three of them were known as the Three Musketeers. Vince shared a story with me that speaks to how these ballers—one from Florida, one from North Carolina (by way of Louisiana), and one from Germany—became true Tar Heel Brothers:

> Every New Year's Eve, Antawn, Ademola, and I would bring the new year in playing one-on-one-on-one. The three of us did this for the three years that we were together. This became our tradition. Each year, the game that meant the most was the one that was being played as the clock struck midnight. That darn Ademola won that game our freshman year. We would for ever hear about that for the rest of the year. The game winning wealth was spread pretty evenly amongst Antawn and I, but it was the win as the clock struck midnight that held the most weight.
>
> What made this so much fun, but still a battle, was that Ademola, Antawn, my childhood friend Cori Brown and I were dorm suite mates as freshmen. Antawn and Ademola were on one side, while, separated by our bathroom, Cori and I were on the other side of the suite. We were always connected. We did everything together. We got along and argued like brothers. We had to practice how to correctly pronounce Ademola Olayiwola Okulaja. Since basketball players came to campus early, we had time to really get to know each other. We were excited about our opportunity to play at UNC. Ademola was a little older than 'Twan and me because in Europe they attend school to grade 13.
>
> Antawn and I left college a year early. Leaving Ademola was one of the things that made my decision to leave tough. With

Antawn and I leaving, it left Ademola with a team that wasn't as good as what we knew in our sophomore and junior years—going to back-to-back NCAA Final Fours.

'Twan, Ademola and I would have night runs to get something to eat. We looked out for each other and supported each other on and off the court. As freshmen, we really had conversations because things on the court were up and down for me. It wasn't long before the controversy started that had Ademola and I in the middle of it. I went from a starter to coming off the bench behind Ademola. People tried to make a competition between us because we sort of played the same position. There were rumors that I wanted to leave UNC. The rumors went as far to say that I was going to Florida with Billy Donovan who was coaching his first year there. I was frustrated with the situation, but I never wanted to leave. I had the support of Ademola and 'Twan. That made it easy for me to stay and get better. I knew I had my best friends' support.

At UNC, freshmen could not have a vehicle on the campus. 'Twan, Ademola and I were picked up in what always seemed like the smallest vehicles. 'Twan and Ademola were 6' 9". I was the short one at 6' 6". Most of the time, I was the one squeezed in the back. Whether in the gym, in the dorm, or in cramped vehicles, we supported each other.

When you are a Tar Heel, you are a member of the family—this is another aspect of the Carolina Way. Amongst basketball teams over the years there develops a special brotherhood that is very close knit. Players and coaches stay in touch with each other, are best men and groomsmen at each other's weddings, become godparents to each other's children, and are even there when a Tar Heel is fallen. At Dean Smith's funeral in 2015, dozens of former players and coaches attended. The Tar Heel family was also to lose Ademola Okulaja in May 2022.

Coach Smith might not have liked some of Vince's crowd-pleasing initiatives, but they didn't affect his game at all. Before Vince arrived at college, in the summer of 1995, Jerry Stackhouse and Rasheed Wallace, UNC's two top starters, made an early exit for the NBA draft. This left a big void on the team, and it necessitated that freshmen Antawn Jamison,

Ademola Okulaja, and Vince became starters from day one. Another element of the Carolina Way is that every person on the team is on the same page. The assistant coaches were direct with Vince and the other freshman starters: *we need you to contribute right away*. There were no politics, just reality.

Assistant coaches at UNC play a vital role in the success of the team and of individual players, on and off the court. They adhere to the Carolina Way and the culture that Dean Smith built. Two of Dean Smith's assistant coaches when Vince played there, Dave Hanners and Phil Ford, later reminisced about Vince and his amazing career at UNC. Dave Hanners wrote this about Vince's skills and character:

> When Vince arrived at UNC as a freshman, his physical abilities were obvious, as were his basketball skills. Looking back, he was gifted as any player we ever had at Carolina. When I think of Vince Carter, I think, "Amazing, unreal"! Why do I say that? Vince played longer in the NBA than any other player.
>
> Vince was a great ambassador for UNC and for his family. We NEVER had better. Vince was unbelievable with the kids [at our basketball summer camp]. He would visit with the campers for hours. They all loved him. Most "stars" do not have time for this sort of thing, but Vince always went beyond the call of duty to make the campers feel special…
>
> Vince was super compassionate and good-hearted. It is a testament to his character and perseverance that Vince became one of the greatest competitors in the history of the NBA. Some players we had at Carolina developed late physically. We labeled these players "late bloomers". Vince was different. He worked hard, listened, took coaching, and developed a great competitive spirit to go along with his superior athletic skills.

Coach Hanners was part of the Carolina family. He had played four varsity seasons as a guard for the Tar Heels from 1972 to 1976, was co-captain in his senior year, and was an assistant coach for many years before Vince arrived. Coach Hanners eventually moved to the NBA, where he spent years as an assistant and developmental coach for teams including the New York Knicks and the New Orleans Pelicans.

Phil Ford was another of the assistant coaches who guided Vince throughout his college basketball career. Coach Ford had played point guard on the UNC team from 1974 to 1978, when he broke many scoring records and led the team to the NCAA Tournament Championship Game. Coach Ford was also a college All-American winner of the prestigious John R. Wooden Award, as well as the #2 pick in the 1979 NBA draft. He won the NBA's coveted Rookie-of-the-Year and had a solid NBA career. In 1976, Phil won an Olympic Gold Medal on a Team USA that was coached by none other than Dean Smith. At time of writing, Phil Ford works for the Educational Foundation, which is the fund-raising arm of the University of North Carolina Athletic Department.

When Vince was in high school, Coach Ford handled most of the recruiting. He made sure it was personal. He spent a lot of time in Volusia County, FL, and could be spotted at Mainland High School games, as well as other area high school basketball games where Vince was playing.

You could even find Phil on the band field watching Vince practice and carry out his duties as drum major of the marching band. Perhaps he was checking out Vince's character. I'm not sure, but I don't know of another coach that watched Vince's band practice.

One sunny afternoon on the Mainland High School band field, Coach Ford was an interested spectator watching the band. If you know anything about Florida weather, it can be sunny one minute and a few minutes later a hellacious thunderstorm will blanket the area. Phil got his up-close and personal taste of Central Florida's sometimes rapidly changing weather. Out of nowhere, several streaks of lightening scrolled across the sky, accompanied by loud booms of thunder. Soon the sky was dark. Since I was the band announcer, I attended practices, too, so that a script could be developed for "the show," our halftime or pep rally performances. I remember that I looked over at Coach Ford as he was leaning on the metal chain-link fence—not the best idea in a lightning storm! Vince repeatedly blew his whistle, yelled "let's go" to the band members, and pointed them towards the band room. As fast as they could with their instruments in tow, band members began running to the band room, away from danger. Coach Ford's head was on a swivel, watching Vince lead the band indoors. As I ran towards the coach, we made eye-contact and I began pointing towards the band room, too. Coach Ford took off running and later admitted that he hadn't known what the heck was going on, but Vince and I had convinced him to go with the crowd. Once we reached the band room, Drum Major Vince explained the danger of being in an open field while lightning is streaking across the sky; not to mention that the coach was leaning on that metal fence. After a few moments of catching our breath, the indoor version of band practice continued.

Years later, Coach Phil Ford had these comments about Vince:

> Of course, selfishly, I wish Vince had stayed at Carolina for four years. One more year of elbowing Dave Hanners and saying, "Can you believe that! Did I see what I think I saw?" It happened over and over again. We knew that what we were seeing did not come along very often. It was like being on the bench at UNC when Michael Jordan was playing. Human highlight reels! I told every NBA scout and every shoe rep: if you want a player that will be remembered as a great NBA player, you better sign Vince Carter.

Vince's high school games certainly impressed the coaching staff of UNC, who trusted him enough to be a starter. Even though he started games, he wasn't playing nearly as many minutes as he had at Mainland, because of the team system that is the crux of the Carolina Way, yet he still contributed greatly to the team's success.

Early in Vince's sophomore season, however, his playing time started decreasing even more. I asked him what was going on; was everything alright? He said everything was fine—but a mom knows. I could hear a contradiction in his voice, and I could see the disappointment on his face during the games.

   In the Carter household, we don't blame others when life is not as we would have it. We assess the problem, come up with a plan to fix it (or at least make it better), and work the plan. Candidly, there were a few conversations that centered around the possibility that UNC might not be the place for Vince. After all, there were 76 other colleges or universities that most likely would still be interested in recruiting him. But Vince loved the University of North Carolina and the Tar Heel basketball family. As members of his own family, we knew that this was the place for him.

   Antawn Jamison became Vince's teammate and best friend at UNC. He remembers Vince feeling homesick during his early time as a Tar Heel. He also remembers Vince, after his summer break in Florida, being "super focused" for his third season. Vince's playing stats reflect this. Each season he improved, to the point that his playing time was 31 minutes per game (out of 40 possible) during his junior year, his final season in college. His average (mean) 15.6 points per game that season were less than they had been in high school, but that's because UNC played structured team ball where no one player dominated. Vince's efficiency that season, however, was incredible! He made 66% of his 2-point shots and 44% of his 3-pointers. That 3-point percentage in particular was remarkable for the time and boded well for his NBA future. I saw him growing as a young man and into an outstanding basketball player.

   During Vince's matriculation year at UNC, he had performed well in the classroom and on the basketball court. I had seen him growing as a young man, and into an outstanding basketball player. It was easy to see that Vince loved being a college athlete. In his three years (1995–98) at UNC, the Tar Heel Basketball Team made it to the NCAA Final Four during his sophomore (RCA Dome, Indianapolis, IN) and junior (Alamodome, San Antonio, TX) years. In both tournaments, Vince played well, and I'm sure many NBA scouts noticed. These were very exciting times. Unfortunately, the Tar Heels did not go on to win the Championship, but it was an amazing ride, done the Carolina Way.

8

Should He Stay or Should He Go? The NBA Draft

In collegiate sports, the opportunity may come for the elite student-athlete to forego some of their college years to test the waters of pro sports. In other words, it may be time for the young athlete to go pro and get paid. Nowadays, there are more pathways for top amateur athletes, including high school and college students, to make money before committing to their sport as a career. That wasn't always so.

When Vince was in college, amateur athletes had zero means to profit from their early sports successes while maintaining their college eligibility. Since the mid-2010s, the NCAA rules have progressed in the right direction—though there is still room for improvement. In 2015, the NCAA created a policy that allowed colleges to pay a "cost of attendance" stipend. As a result, most prominent NCAA Division 1 athletic programs started to provide their scholarship student-athletes with small stipends for such expenses as books, gas, or other costs they incur. The amounts of these stipends were modest and were more proportionate to a part-time "work–study" program than to a full-time job.

Now, in the 2020s, athletes can also earn money using their "Name, Image, Likeness" (NIL) to sell merchandise and ink media deals while still retaining college eligibility. This is a real boon to elite and popular high school and college athletes, especially those from lower-income homes. After all, these young athletes work hard and entertain an audience, often a paying audience—so why shouldn't they benefit? Some critics would perhaps protest that these are student-athletes getting a free education through their scholarships. To this, I would counter that if we consider the cost of a four-year academic degree at university and compare that with the millions of dollars that the university makes from sales of sporting event tickets, endorsements, TV rights, sales of jerseys and of balls and other memorabilia, there is a massive surplus.

I do have one concern, though, about the new-found ability of students to monetize their success. It is that there doesn't appear to be a cap on the amount of money a student-athlete can now make. Too much money in the hands of anyone who is not mature enough to handle it can be problematic and potentially disastrous.

There was absolutely nothing along the lines of "cost of attendance" stipends, let alone NIL, when Vince was in college. You were either a pro or you weren't. Any minor transaction, like, say, bartering autographed merchandise—perhaps a game-worn jersey—for free meals at a restaurant, were strictly prohibited. You could lose your NCAA eligibility, and for something as simple as that your athletic scholarship would be in jeopardy. Some athletes lost scholarships for NCAA transgressions that were far more trivial than this example. The rules were unfairly restrictive—and seemed to be enforced way more in sports dominated by African American athletes; but that's another discussion.

Because there was no way a college athlete could earn money *and* remain eligible, there was an underground economy back then. Shady people offered money, cars, or other favors to top athletes if they would play for a preferred college team. Back then, even I, as Vince's parent, was offered nice, expensive things by a few dubious entities. They were not very subtle. But we were not interested! Vince's bonus dad and I were both teachers, and we were careful with money. We were by no means rich, but we lived in a very nice 4,500 sq. ft. home in a very pleasant upscale neighborhood. During high school, Vince had his own car, his own large bedroom, the latest computer, and everything else a high school boy reasonably needed. Therefore, Vince was somewhat insulated from temptation. Imagine, though, if he had not had these things, how tempting it would have been.

On our first visit to the University of North Carolina, we were informed by coaches that the only two things Vince would get for playing basketball there were an opportunity for a great education and the opportunity to play Tar Heel basketball. They made it clear that they did not, in any way, bribe athletes, or their parents, or high school coaches. This was a principle of the Carolina Way. I appreciated this, along with the assurance that no one else on the team was bought and paid for. That was an indication that Vince's teammates were there because they truly wanted to play for Coach Dean Smith and get a world-class education, and for no other reason.

It was not lost on Vince and his teammates, however, that if you were a star player on the Tar Heel Basketball Team you could make some serious money by declaring for the NBA draft. If a baller was selected in the NBA lottery, which UNC basketball players often were, they might literally become a millionaire overnight. In fact, the two upper classmen players who declared for the NBA draft just before Vince started at UNC—Jerry Stackhouse and Rasheed Wallace—were both selected in the lottery, and both became millionaires within a very short space of time.

In the 1995 NBA draft, Rasheed was selected #4 overall, and his first-year salary was around $1.5 million (or $3 million in the early 2020s, adjusted for inflation). Jerry was picked #3 in the same draft and earned a starting rookie salary of nearly $2 million (or $4 million in the early 2020s). These figures only represent the first year's payout on their rookie contracts. Both had plenty more money guaranteed to come over the next few years. I'm sure these rookie salary numbers were tempting for Vince, as was the excitement and allure of becoming part of an NBA team.

With Vince, I could see that he was in a quandary trying to decide whether to forego his senior year of college and declare himself eligible for the NBA draft. He knew he was good, but was he lottery-pick good? Was he ready for the pros? I have always prided myself on—if not having the answer—being able to research and find the answer for my son. This time, I was not so sure. After all, this was the first rodeo for all of us. It became my mission to provide my son with the best information about his draft prospects.

Here was the reality check. As mentioned, the odds against a student-athlete achieving a professional sport career are astronomically high. Approximately 1% of NCAA men's basketball players and 2% of NCAA football players are drafted by NBA or NFL teams. Even if the student-athlete is drafted, that is no assurance of a successful professional career. If an athlete's sole objective is to make the pros, and they do not get drafted, then they suddenly find themselves in a world that demands skills they may not possess. Those who are not successful in their quest for a professional sports career, having completed only one year of college as a stepping stone to the chance to be a pro, often find themselves out of the pro sport with no degree, very little to no money, and no answer to how they will live a comfortable life. The odds of "one and done" are high stakes.

In 1998, the first 13 players chosen in the NBA draft were considered lottery picks. The teams that had the worst 13 records during the NBA season were the teams that received the top 13 draft picks. There was a luck-of-the-draw ping-pong ball style draft lottery event that determined the order that the lottery teams made their selections. If an athlete was selected in the lottery, they were guaranteed a multi-year contract that would pay them millions. The higher their selection, or closer they were to the top pick, the more money they earned.

In the NBA, however (unlike in the NFL), the money was guaranteed for the length of a player's rookie contract. This meant the player would get paid the full value of the contract no matter what, even if they didn't perform as expected or in the event of a career-ending injury. After the term of the rookie contract ended, the team that drafted the player could decide to extend the contract or decline it. If it was extended, the player usually received a substantial raise. If it was declined, the player was free to sign with another team but generally earned less guaranteed money. But those lottery rookie contracts still guaranteed millions, per the NBA salary scale.

After I started to research the draft, the decision became quite simple to me. If Vince was going to be a lottery pick, then I would advise him to leave school and enter the NBA draft. If it didn't look as if he would be in the top 13, I would advise him to stay. After all, Vince loved being a college student. He loved every aspect of student life outside the gym, including his classes, his friendships, and playing the role of the "Big Man on Campus."

With my research, I was determined to figure out where Vince would most likely go in the draft by approaching the experts in the field, or at least the ones I had access to. I have always had the mindset to work my way from the top down. That just seemed to be the most expeditious way to get answers. Our first consultation was with Dean Smith, Bill Guthridge and Phil Ford, the UNC coaches. I recall Coach Smith making a chart of pros (reasons to stay) and cons (reasons to go) on the board. There were two reasons for Vince to stay and eight reasons for him to go. Coach Smith turned to us and said, "He is ready". I greatly appreciated his honesty, and I know Vince did, too. I still thought it was wise to go outside the UNC bubble to gather more expert opinions though.

A few of the college coaches that I developed relationships with during Vince's recruiting process had made their way into various positions in the NBA. To make sure I had the best information, I reached out to one of them, R.C. Buford, to get his opinion on whether he thought the time was right for Vince to make the jump.

Today, R.C. is the chief executive officer of San Antonio Spurs Sports and Entertainment. He's done extremely well with the Spurs, having been a key part of the team that selected basketball greats such as Manu Ginobili, Tony Parker, and Kawhi Leonard, to name a few. During R.C.'s tenure with the Spurs, the team has won five NBA titles, four of which were won when R.C. was the team's general manager.

During Vince's college recruiting process, R.C. was an assistant coach with the University of Florida. We had the pleasure of getting to know him then. Around the time Vince was considering the draft, R.C. had taken a role as a scout for the Spurs. I knew it was his job to understand which college student-athletes were ready to play in the NBA. So, I called him about Vince's prospects. He was upfront. He strongly believed that Vince would be selected in the lottery, probably closer to the top lottery than last. The Spurs did not have a lottery pick in this draft. Therefore, he knew Vince's name would be called long before their selection. Again, I truly appreciated his input.

Next, I called the NBA. Yes, I contacted the NBA office in New York. I explained the nature of my call and was directed to Rod Thorn, a former NBA player and head coach. At the time of my call, Rod Thorn was the NBA's Executive Vice President of Basketball Operations. Though Mr. Thorn did not tell me whether Vince should go or stay, he did share with me the League's projection for Vince if he decided to enter the draft. The projection was in the top half of the lottery. Unofficially, he quipped that "Vince will be gone before 8, even if it's posthumously." I got a good chuckle out of that. Mr. Thorn is a funny man.

I hope that today it is common for the agents and parents of top NBA prospects to contact the League directly in regard to their athlete's potential draft order. Back in the mid-1990s, however, this was not common, or so Mr. Thorn told me. He also said he wished more parents were proactive this way: some would benefit from reassurance it was the right move for their son, while others needed a reality check.

These expert opinions, from Vince's college coaches, a team scout, and the NBA itself, formed a barometer that together indicated to me that, unless Vince really screwed up or sustained a serious injury, he would make the team and would have a chance at a lasting career in the NBA. It also indicated that he was heavily favored to be a draft lottery pick.

With the best information on hand, Vince decided to forego his senior year as a student-athlete at the University of North Carolina. This also meant this would break up his group of close friends, which made it a very hard choice for Vince. If Antawn and he stayed, he knew how much promise the 1998 Tar Heel team had. Vince described the hard part of his decision like this:

> Antawn and I left college a year early. Leaving Ademola was one of the things that made the decision to leave tough. It left Ademola with a team that wasn't as good as what we knew in our sophomore and junior years, going back-to-back NCAA Final Fours. We still talk about our time at UNC today.

The decision was made. The three Musketeers would go their separate ways, but their deep trust and shared friendship remained steadfast—until the sad loss of Ademola in May 2022.

Making the enormous life-changing decision to go pro is stressful and emotional for a student-athlete and their friends and family. As a parent you may feel like a yo-yo with the ups and downs of it all. I handled this uncertainty with prayer, the knowledge I gained from my research, and common sense. I bounced a lot of my novice questions and concerns off my husband, who was as eager to do right by Vince as I was. Together, we advised Vince using all the knowledge, wisdom, and ethics we had.

One would hope that those who love, and are advising, a student-athlete are doing so with no ulterior motive. In other words, the advisers should not be acting in their own self-interest at all. Sadly, there are cases where parents' or advisers' self-interest does take precedence. Parents and other family members may pressure their student-athletes to take the highest offer because it benefits their family members as much as the young athlete. For the best chance of success, the student-athlete, with the help of advisers, must make the decision that is best for him or her on a personal level.

In the spring of 1998, around the time Vince decided to go pro, he asked me if I would consider retiring from my position as an educator to manage his NBA career. I hold a Bachelor of Science degree in Business Education, a Master of Science degree in Administration and Supervision, and a Doctorate in Business Administration. In my 21-year teaching career I taught subjects such as business law, accounting, business math, business communications, keyboarding and data processing. Therefore, I had a strong foundation in the management and administration side of things. Nevertheless, my learning curve was still quite steep. None of my education or teaching experiences covered overseeing the success of a professional athlete. So I knew I needed to start by finding Vince representation—the best agent I could find.

Most people have absolutely no experience in hiring an

agent or representation for a student-athlete hopeful of entering the professional sports ranks. So what does one look for in this type of representation? Once again, research and common sense helped. We wanted an agency that was well established in the professional sports management industry and had a track record of success. It didn't matter whether the lead agent was male or female, Black, Caucasian, or other. It did matter that the agent and the company had connections—not only connections in the sports world but also a reach into various marketing agencies. It is the opinion of many people, including me, that Vince Carter has a million-dollar smile. I believed that there was an opportunity for Vince to have endorsement deals along with his NBA contract.

If you are the parent of a talented athlete and there is no one in the student-athlete's camp that is familiar with accounting principles or investment strategy, I recommend you hire a financial management person who is separate from the management agent. This creates a system of checks and balances. In other words, the management team checks the financial team, and the financial team checks the management team.

Again, I stress that there must also be a person with absolutely no ulterior motives who is making sure that everything that is done is in the best interests of the athlete. In Vince's case, that person was, and still is, me. One tip I learned from Oprah Winfrey that has served me well over time was to have all documents from financial institutions sent directly to me. Of course, the accountant needs this information too, and receives copies of everything, but I make sure that I receive the originals.

With the guidance of Vince's bonus dad and me, Vince interviewed several sports agents in our home. We required the prospective agents to travel in person to us. This was the best way to gauge our comfort level in relation to their organizations, as well as their potential commitment to us. After all, your home is your comfort zone. If the potential agent is not willing to make a personal trip for a prime potential client, then he/she is probably not worth hiring. After a lot of research and discussions, we decided that agent William "Tank" Black and the PMI firm would be the choice to guide us through Vince's NBA career.

After the agent was decided, I learned that if the prospective professional athlete's draft projection is admirable, banks and other lending institutions will offer them cash advances. This also depends on the rapport that the agent has built with the company. After all, the world knows where top college athletes will probably be drafted.

Like most young athletes, Vince wanted a new vehicle. I suppose that the 1996 Ford Explorer that he was driving was not representative of a soon-to-be NBA basketball player. So, he purchased a beautiful 1999 Lincoln Navigator. Of course, Vince wanted to look dapper for his big night, too. His new agent informed us that Elevee Custom Wear, in California, was popular amongst professional athletes. We soon understood why. The staff of this custom clothing store flew to Florida to measure Vince for a few suits and accessories. I believe that if you look good, you feel good. Vince's draft night apparel proved this to be true.

Soon, all of Team Carter was in place. This professional support group for Vince included his agent, William "Tank" Black (PMI), the public relations firm of Michael and Kathy Butler, Vince, and me. There were both a legal counsel and an accountant within the PMI group, who handled contracts and financial matters. The instructions from Vince were that each member of Team Carter report to me. That meant *everything* came across my desk for scrutiny and approval. Believe me, many athletes don't have someone they absolutely trust handling their affairs. As a result, they are either taken advantage of or miss key opportunities. I made sure that these things never happened to Vince.

To stay on top of things, and to reduce the depth of my

learning curve, there were many meetings. I learned how professional sports, particularly basketball, operated and how to trust my own team. The members of Team Carter were instructed to keep me abreast of everything, including the good, the bad, and the ugly. They, in turn, learned to trust me as well. We were fortunate that Vince always showed common sense, always thought before he spoke or acted, and is genuinely a smart and good person. Over the years, Team Carter had minimal bad news to report, and one scandal involving a member of Team Carter. More on this later. Our cohesion as a team allowed Vince to focus on what he did best: play basketball.

In preparation for the 1998 NBA draft, Vince worked out for a few NBA teams, including the Denver Nuggets, the Toronto Raptors, the Golden State Warriors, the Sacramento Kings, the Dallas Mavericks, and the (now defunct) Vancouver Grizzlies. As the dust settled and NBA media analysts got involved, Vince was projected to go to the Toronto Raptors with the fourth pick in the draft. I am proud to say this mirrored the predictions that resulted from my research, which had also told me to be prepared for multiple outcomes. I knew that Vince could potentially be living in a variety of cities and we ought not to get too invested in any one outcome. The important part was for Vince and me to enjoy the experience. This was a good approach—considering that fate threw us some extra chaos on draft night.

In 1998, the NBA draft was held in Vancouver, British Columbia, in Canada, at the Rogers Arena. Everything just seemed to be purposefully coming together. Vince was nervous but looked awesome in his new custom-tailored suit. For me, nervous was an understatement. By this time, we knew that Vince would probably be drafted with the fourth pick by the Toronto Raptors, an NBA basketball team in Canada. This was our first trip to British Columbia, so we arrived a couple of days in advance to get acclimated and ready for what was no doubt a monumental day in Vince's life.

Every intelligence we had prior to the draft indicated that Vince would go with the fourth pick to the Toronto Raptors, but fate had other ideas. On Draft Day, 1998, David Stern, Commissioner of the NBA, announced that "with the fourth pick, the Toronto Raptors select Antawn Jamison." *What?!* Vince's college teammate, Antawn Jamison, going to the Toronto Raptors! We (and by "we" I mean Vince and his entire team) were in shock. Vividly I recall the moment immediately after the announcement of the pick when Mr. Jamison (Antawn's father) and I made eye contact. He looked confused—and so was I. Watching the NBA staff hand each member of the Jamison party a Toronto Raptors cap was surreal.

Approximately five minutes later, NBA Commissioner David Stern announced that "with the fifth pick in the NBA draft, the Golden State Warriors select Vince Carter." Team Carter was baffled! I recall being totally confused when, moments later, members of the Carter party received the Warriors cap. My brain was on overdrive calculating the travel math. I thought, "Well, this might not be bad at all. We have family in the Oakland area of California." Next thought was, "Gosh, the east coast to west coast flights are going to be a killer, but I guess we will get accustomed to it."

As my brain was scrambling, Commissioner Stern made yet another announcement. There was a trade between the Golden State Warriors and the Toronto Raptors. The two friends, Antawn and Vince, were traded for each other. As if it was scripted, everyone from the Jamison table and everyone from the Carter table got up and exchanged caps. I don't like drama, and decided that this bit of craziness would be enough for me, thank you.

After the drama of draft night, the excitement of Vince being in the NBA was building to a "pinch me" high. The day after the draft, Team Carter flew to Toronto to meet with the Raptors' general manager, Glen Grunwald, coach Butch Carter, other members of the basketball staff, and some

Raptors fans (more on this later). After the introductions and press conference, other less public basketball-related matters were discussed. For us, this was an opportunity to ask about housing and vehicles, and learn where the grocery store was located. Of course, I wanted to know the location of the best mall. I was told it was the Eaton Center, and I gave it an "A" grade. Learning about our new home away from home would be another steep learning curve for Vince and me.

Toronto is virtually a city underground, and the shopping is amazing! We discovered that Canadian money is far different from that of the United States. There are loonies ($1.00 coins) and toonies ($2.00). It was also most important that Vince and I learned the Canadian National Anthem. After all, along with the anthem of the United States, it would be sung at all the Raptors' home and away games. Vince could not wait to represent his new city, fans and country in the NBA. He made quite a splash.

The Making of Vince Carter

9

From Rookie to Vinsanity

Vince's draft night had taken place June 24th, 1998, in Vancouver, British Columbia, Canada, where, as mentioned, he was selected with the fifth pick by the Golden State Warriors and then, moments after the pick was announced, traded to the Toronto Raptors. Since we were already in Canada, this made it a little easier for us to visit our new home city and team right away. The day after the draft, Vince, Harry, and I flew on a private jet across the vast expanse of greater Canada to Toronto. I remember how excited Vince was to take part in his first official Raptors press conference, jersey photo shoot and other team events. He had participated in press conferences and photo shoots before, but never as a professional athlete.

Vince had already met with the team for his pre-draft workout, but this was my first trip to the city that would become my home base for the next few years. We were still feeling the high of draft night as we flew in that sleek jet, giddy with the knowledge that Vince had made it to the NBA.

Once we landed in Toronto, we were driven to a premium hotel that had a sky bridge connecting it to the arena where the Raptors played. There was so much excitement surrounding Vince from the moment we arrived. We met with top team brass, including the general manager Glen Grunwald, the head coach Butch Carter (no relation) and other key team people. We enjoyed meeting everyone.

During this time, the Raptors was a very new NBA franchise, as they had been founded only three years earlier, in 1995. But their fan base was already rock solid and passionate. As you might expect, if you follow the team, Raptors super fan Nav Batia met Vince on that day one in Toronto. Nav was introduced to us by the executives of the Raptors organization, who already held him in high regard. Many non-Raptor basketball fans know of Nav too, as he's the Sikh gentleman in the turban who sits courtside for every single Raptors home game. During games, Nav frequently stands up and leads the crowds in cheers, or urges the players on. He's as much of a fixture at home games as their official team mascot, the red dinosaur "raptor." Nav remembers being part of a contingent of passionate Raptors fans who crossed the skybridge from the hotel to the arena to greet their new rookie, Vince Carter. Nav told me fans had been so incredibly stoked that the team ended up with Vince via their draft night trade.

A deep friendship between me and Nav began from my first day in Toronto. Sometimes in life you meet someone, and even though you don't know a thing about them, you just click on all levels. That was Nav and me. From the moment I met him, I found him so kind; he said the nicest things, like, "If there's anything I can do for you or your son, just let me know." He meant every word of it, too. Nav was extremely helpful to us as he made sure that we had transportation— really nice cars—to move around his beautiful city. To this day, Nav is the most passionate sports fan that I have ever met in any sport. In fact, he is such an involved, loyal fan that he was the very first "super fan" inducted (2021) into the Naismith Memorial Basketball Hall of Fame. Think of that—the Basketball Hall of Fame! He is really a hardcore Raptors fan. The League got that decision exactly right.

From the start of our time in Toronto, Nav graciously helped us with securing vehicles, becoming generally acclimated and learning where things like the best restaurants and shops were. Whenever Vince or I needed something, Nav was there for us. It was great having someone to call about any issue or need.

While learning the layout of Toronto, I got lost quite a bit. Back then there was no GPS, and one day I got really lost. Knowing Toronto as I do now, I still don't know where in the city I was on that day! Feeling confused, I called Vince, who said, "Don't panic: look for the CN tower—it's very tall. You know to move in that direction." Thankfully for me, in 1998 there weren't as many tall buildings in downtown Toronto as there are now. So, I easily located the CN tower, pointing high above the city, which led me back home. After I was home safely, Vince told me, in his confident and reassuring way, "the best way to learn your way is to get lost." Which was good advice for the start of Vince's NBA career, too, as we had to navigate some seriously unexpected events.

Between the summer of 1998 and mid-January 1999, the NBA was involved in a total work stoppage. There was a lockout because the NBA team owners and the players' union, the NBPA (National Basketball Players Association) couldn't agree on a new contract. In other words, there was a serious disagreement amongst the two parties about player compensation and other key contract terms, which led to the lockout. Before this, the NBA was the only major sports league in the United States where there had never been work stoppage that resulted in cancelled games and a shorter season. That record now ended.

Among other critical aspects of the lockout, players were not permitted at any of the NBA team facilities, nor could they work out with team coaches and trainers. This lockout meant Vince Carter's NBA start was frozen for the foreseeable future. This was my introduction to managing Vince's sports career—months of not knowing what to expect and doing our best.

Vince was so eager to start playing for the Toronto Raptors: the waiting was excruciating. During these months, I tried to keep Vince focused on other things. I purchased furniture for his beautiful rented condo that prominently overlooked the stunning Lake Ontario. Vince and I are both native Floridians, so I knew we both needed to shop for warm clothes. Winter coats, scarves, hats and other items were purchased. We would soon learn how brutal the Canadian winters were, compared with sunny Florida! Once all the boxes were checked for Vince to start his new job in his new city, we waited—and waited. Vince did his best to stay in shape and worked out on his own, but it wasn't the same as an organized team practice with NBA-level coaches and trainers. We were just thankful the lockout hadn't started before the draft.

Prior to the lockout, it had been business as usual for all thirty NBA teams, including the way they approached the draft. In their draft preparation, teams had invited the top college and international prospective players to try out and work out for them in person. These invitations were extended to most top college players who had declared for the draft. You could get an idea of where a player would be selected in the draft based on which teams were inviting him to try out for them. Both Vince and I had been thrilled when he received invitations from many teams that had high lottery picks, including the Raptors. Evaluating the position and needs of the teams that invited Vince to try out had been part of my lottery research.

Because Vince had been continuing his college education and taking classes, submitting homework and taking tests, it had made scheduling his NBA tryouts a little bit of a challenge. It had been my responsibility to coordinate tryouts for Vince, so I'd had to schedule around his academic calendar. In the Carter household, tryouts would not supersede exams or other critical tasks relating to his studies.

Vince's very last pre-draft tryout had been with the Toronto Raptors. The Raptors possessed the #4 pick in the 1998 draft, near the top of the lottery. The Raptors had been anxious to schedule Vince's tryout and team workout, but I had struggled to find the couple of free days in Vince's schedule as requested. After I had talked with people associated with the team, the message was sent to me that if Vince was on the draft board at #4 he would be a Raptor. I got the feeling that this was the code for "with or without a workout," but both Vince and I still felt that a workout with the team was crucial. He wanted to show all interested teams what he could do in person, especially those teams with high draft picks.

The Raptors workout was finally scheduled right before the draft. Vince's flight to Toronto, however, was seriously delayed. He arrived at his hotel, famished, in the wee hours of the morning. Of course, room service was closed, but the hotel staff managed to pull together a little something for the hungry young man to eat. Vince said he had the feeling that everyone at the hotel knew why he was there, and they were all very accommodating.

Not only had the flight been late, but Vince had landed at the airport without his luggage. His workout clothes, including his all-important sneakers, had not arrived with him. The Raptors staff had provided him with workout clothes and shoes. Vince told me he had not been sure how well he would perform on very little sleep, and without the shoes he was accustomed to, for this critical workout.

Predictably, his workout had not been ideal. He told me that "things did not go to his liking." He was disgusted with the number of short jumpers, and even a couple of layups, that he missed. Layups? Yes, he missed layups. It had been a long time since I had seen my son miss a layup. Quite frankly, it had been a long time since I'd seen Vince miss an in-game dunk, so the missed layout news was troubling. The Raptors, unlike Vince, had no post-workout concerns however. According to the Raptors' general manager Glen Grunwald and the head coach Butch Carter, Vince Carter was their guy, and no missed layups would change this. Glen Grunwald commented that Vince's workout was one of the best he had seen. Craig Neal, an assistant coach at that time, told Vince directly that if he was on the board for the fourth pick, he would be a Raptor. Coach Neal said, "you are that good." They marveled over Vince's athleticism, basketball IQ and overall basketball skills—even in borrowed shoes and with minimal rest.

After hearing Vince's scouting report of the Raptors, and the many positive indications he received, I had known that declaring for the draft was the right decision. This reassured me that Vince would be chosen at #4 in the draft if he wasn't selected before that. I could finally relax. But this was the reason our family was so confused at first when Toronto selected Antawn Jamison with the #4 pick. Antawn had not worked out for the Raptors and Vince had. I'm sure Vince had communicated to Antawn some of the things the Raptors told him, like how interested they were in drafting him after his workout. The two young friends didn't hide information from each other. Although they were actually competing against each other in the same draft, their friendship always came first. They supported each other's professional ambitions first, no matter what.

After the draft, the lockout went on longer than we, or anyone in the league or media, expected. Since Vince had foregone his senior year in college, he still needed around a year's worth of credits to graduate. I knew that after his NBA career started it would probably be harder for him to find time to take college classes. This was, after all, before online classes were popular.

I thought back to the simple contract Vince had signed on the napkin in the long car ride to Chapel Hill years before—that he would one day return to college to complete his undergraduate degree. Though he was still a very young adult, I knew he was a man of his word. So, I approached him about using this sudden unexpected free time to pursue some of those outstanding college credits. In short, I suggested he attend summer school at UNC. Vince was hesitant about my back-to-school idea. After all, he was now suddenly wealthy and becoming a sports celebrity. He was also in the process of mentally transitioning from college student to professional athlete, so his initial reluctance was understandable. He used the excuse that summer sessions had already started back at his college, therefore it was too late for him to take classes.

I knew, however, that although the UNC's summer term "A" session was ending, there was another session after it. I told him, "Well you can still attend summer session B". Yes, I did pressure him a little. But in all fairness, at that time the negotiations between the NBA and the NBPA were at a near-total standstill. It did not seem likely that there would be any movement on the contract front until the summer ended, and it was closer to the start of the team's fall training camp. We were both optimistic, as was the rest of Team Carter, that the players and team owners would reconcile their issues before the official NBA season started. After all, there had never been even a single NBA game cancelled because of contract issues… yet. But the summer was clearly going to be a wash for the League.

Vince followed my advice and agreed to go back to school. He made the best of this unexpected lull and flew back to summer school in Chapel Hill. It was also probably mentally healthy for him as well to be back among his UNC friends and teammates, far away from the anxieties of being in a new city, wondering when your new job is going to start. Being back with his team and coaches also helped him stay in shape. As was his habit, whenever he wasn't in class or studying he spent much of the day in the gym.

Finally, in mid-January 1999, the players were called back to work. That's right, the league missed the entire fall 1998 season! The NBA lockout lasted an agonizing, and unprecedented, total of 204 days. We were starting to wonder if they'd be crazy enough scrap the whole season. So my suggestion had proved timely, to say the least.

Vince and I were so relieved he would finally get to work. I was also so proud of him for having made the extra effort to continue his education over the summer. I now knew, in my heart, that he would follow through on the informal contract he had signed on that napkin all those years ago in the car. I knew he'd finish his degree at UNC some day. Little did I suspect, however, that there was drama ahead in relation to this.

There were numerous downsides to the long NBA lockout. It meant a shorter NBA regular season, of 50 games instead of the typical 82. Therefore, Vince's rookie season would be much shorter than usual; but in a way this shortened rookie year for Vince was a blessing in disguise. It made the transition from a college basketball schedule (of approximately 35 games) to a NBA schedule (of approximately 90 games) much easier.

Another result of the lockout was that Vince didn't get to experience a full training camp or play in as many preseason games. The schedule of both training camp and the pre-season were significantly shortened, which meant Vince and the other rookies would have less time to get acclimated to their new teams.

When the lockout ended, we were both so excited that Vince was finally going to get to play basketball with his new team.

The Raptors initially played their home games in Toronto at a place called the Sky Dome, now renamed the Rogers Centre. The Sky Dome was not the ideal venue for basketball, especially not at professional level. It was an enormous stadium with a retractable roof, better suited for baseball (the Toronto Blue Jays also play there), or rock concerts. The interior of the venue was vast, the on-court acoustics were terrible, and the crowd seating was much further away from the court than usual. There was a visible span of darkness behind each basket before the start of the seating rows began. Watching games from the stands, it appeared like the players shot into a black hole. This was not ideal.

Lucky for us, it wasn't long before the amazing Air Canada Centre, now renamed the Scotiabank Arena, became the new home of the Raptors. The Air Canada Centre (ACC), although still large, was smaller and more intimate than the Rogers Centre. It was the perfect home for NBA games. Many fans would come to call it "the house that Vince built."

As mentioned, Butch Carter was the head coach of the Toronto Raptors when Vince started his first full-time job as a professional basketball player. I depended on Butch to make sure that his highly sought-after first round draft pick would be alright in this tough profession. Butch was the perfect coach for young players who needed to be shown the ins and outs of the NBA. He taught players how to be professionals, and nurtured them when times were tough.

One of the first major decisions that Butch needed to make was which position Vince should play. Vince was a versatile player. He could play point guard, shooting guard, and—at a bit over 6'6"—he could even play the small forward role when needed. Butch and his coaches decided to place Vince at the big (shooting) guard position. This position was ideal for a born dunker and scorer.

It allowed Vince to show off his considerable skills from his very first game. If Vince had been playing at the point guard position, he probably wouldn't have gotten to dunk and show off as often. So, making Vince the team's starting shooting guard was perfect.

Also on Vince's first team was our cousin Tracy McGrady.

The Making of Vince Carter

Tracy had left high school to enter the 1997 NBA draft, where he was selected by the Raptors with the #9 pick. We didn't always know that Tracy was family. Believe it or not, it was only in the year before Vince was drafted that the two young men figured out they were cousins. This happened while Vince was a student-athlete at UNC and Tracy was attending high school nearby in Durham, North Carolina, at Mount Zion Academy. Tracy, like Vince, was originally from Central Florida. Tracy's family was from Auberndale, part of the greater Orlando area. Tracy would come to the Dean Dome in Chapel Hill during open court sessions to play basketball. He was one of the top high school players in the nation, so he was already an extremely skilled player, of course. When Tracy came to open practice, often the Tar Heel basketball players would join in the fun and challenge him to some pickup basketball. Vince and Tracy got to know each other from engaging in many pickup games, but they still didn't know that they were related.

One day, Tracy had asked Vince if he could leave some of his basketball items in his locker, because he was going to a family reunion and would not be around for the weekend. Just before this, Vince had been speaking with me on the phone, when I had told him that my mom, Peggy Green, was also going to a family reunion that weekend. Baba, Vince's pet name for his grandmother, was so excited about getting together with family. My mom loved family reunions.

At the festivities, my mom was telling everyone who would listen about her grandson, Vincent, who played for the University of North Carolina. Tracy was in earshot of this conversation and interrupted my mom, saying, "Wait a minute, Cousin Peggy! Vince Carter, who plays basketball at UNC is your grandson? I just left him." Tracy continued, "so, Vince Carter is my cousin?" It was a shocking, but wonderful, revelation. My mom and I could not wait to tell Vince how they had put two and two together. At the next family reunion, both Vince and Tracy attended as fellow Raptors.

What are the chances? The family had a blast, as we were all beaming with pride.

The start of Vince's NBA career was a revelation. By now you know that I'm a proud mama, and you might expect me to say that. But even I was startled by how quickly Vince and his game adapted to the League. There was no adjustment period. He was high flying and dunking from his very first game.

Vince's first NBA game was an away game where the Raptors played the Boston Celtics, in Boston. Boston's basketball arena was called the Boston Garden back then and it was known to be a fairly inhospitable place for visiting teams and players. To this day, the Garden (now named the TD Garden) is purported to have the worst locker room facilities for visiting teams. It wasn't any better back then. Vince, however, didn't care about the crummy locker room or jeering Boston fans. During the game, the Raptors' forward, veteran NBA player Charles Oakley, saw the rookie open on his right side and tossed up a lob that Vince slammed home for the score, like he was born to dunk. Just like that, "Vinsanity" was born.

"Vinsanity" was the term NBA fans would come to use to describe the phenomenon that is Vince Carter playing ball at his vigorous best. "Vinsanity" wasn't just based on the amazing dunks that Vince was capable of. Vince was a great passer, defender and showman. He was the total package. His enthusiasm was infectious—I marveled at his ability to get his teammates and fans pumped up. I loved watching the crowd go crazy over my son. It was wonderful seeing Vince's fans in the Mainland gym—this had been true at the Dean Dome at UNC, too, but seeing it happen at a packed NBA arena was unreal. I'd also get to watch my new friend Nav go crazy for Vince as he cheered from his court-side seat. He rooted for Vince like he was family, too, which he basically was.

Nav remembers when Vince came to town and how unreal it was. He loved watching Vince's seemingly impossible dunks and other heroic on-court moves. Nav has reminisced that Vince provided "a different thing every night." You'd see a show and be asking yourself, "how did he do that?" Nav explained that many new Canadian fans went to their first basketball game ever just to see Vince play; that Vince enlivened the city of Toronto and gave sports fans new hope. Nav would even watch the highlights after each game—something he hadn't done before Vince showed up.

While Toronto fell in love with Vince, I fell in love with Toronto. It was my thought that Vince would play there for his entire career. In my naivety, I didn't realize that a player staying with one team throughout what is hoped to be a long career was not common. Nevertheless, I wanted to get involved in the community. So, I asked my new best friend Nav for guidance. Nav, as always, was eager to help me. Once I got to know him, along with the people at the Raptors Foundation, I began to do what I could to encourage kids and help families where I could.

Each NBA team has prescribed team and individual appearance assignments for the players. Vince was off making his appearances, and I had mine too. I read to children in schools and libraries. I love to help kids learn.

In 1998, Vince and I founded a charity to help those in need, called Embassy of Hope Foundation, which is still in full operation today. Back then, along with the Raptors Foundation and a little help from Nav, the Embassy of Hope Foundation hosted Christmas parties for low-income families. We provided food baskets, gifts for the entire family, a scrumptious lunch, and a visit from Santa and the Raptor. You know what's better than Santa to kids? Santa and a dinosaur.

It also didn't take long for us to decide to hold summer basketball camps, called the Vince Carter Youth Basketball Academy, in Toronto. We had to hold double sessions to accommodate the 500+ young ballers that we hosted. I am proud to say that several of the current Canadian NBA players attended Vince's basketball academy. Also during the summer, Vince hosted the Vince Carter Charity Basketball game. This was a weekend of fun for invited NBA players to play pickup basketball for a great cause. This game would boast sellout crowds to raise money to help people in need in the community.

Vince graciously lent his name and time to host fundraisers for other organizations too. One such event was the Vince Carter Charity Golf Tournament. The proceeds went to the Raptors Foundation, to assist them in the exemplary work that they were doing throughout the greater Toronto area.

Meanwhile, Vince kept doing his thing on court. Vinsanity was as much a statement for the Raptors and Canadian basketball as it was for Vince himself. Vince made an impact in his rookie season, averaging 18.3 points and 5.7 rebounds per game. Even with the shortened season of 50 games, the team won more games than they had in the previous year. They finished with a season record of 23–27. Not quite a winning season yet, but still a big improvement over the previous year. They were on their way. After the season ended, Vince was voted the NBA's Rookie-of-the-Year for the 1998–99 season. He may have been drafted #5, but he finished the season #1 among rookies.

Vinsanity started as a Toronto phenomenon, but it soon spread league-wide after Vince's All-Star appearances. He became known for his spectacular dunking during the All-Star weekend slam dunk contest. Vince's dunks were spectacular! Many consider him the best dunker ever in the NBA to this day.

Vince's high flying and dunking play style attracted new fans from all across the NBA and the world. In his second season with the Raptors, Vince led the Raptors to their first ever playoff appearance, with guidance from veteran players Dell Curry, Charles Oakley, Mugsy Bogues, and Kevin Willis.

Meanwhile, Vince's cousin Tracy was coming into his own too, transitioning from a bench player to an elite starter. Tracy flourished alongside Cousin Vince.

Vince's entry into the NBA was a high-flying spectacle. Vince was so proud to help put the Raptors on the map, and Canada truly appreciated Vince. He earned so many amazing nicknames—not just the informal V or VC, but also Florida Flash, Air Canada, Half Man and Half Amazing; and of course there was Vinsanity. The Raptors broke the NBA League attendance records in 2000, 2001, and 2002. Not only was the Air Canada Centre sold out night after night, but arenas throughout the NBA reported their highest number of spectators whenever Vince Carter came to town.

10

For the Record— What Happened in Toronto

As you can imagine, Vinsanity was an amazing ride not just for Vince, but for me and the rest of our family. Being part of the Raptors family, and being so welcomed and appreciated by the fans, is something that will always make us happy and proud. From the start, Vince was very excited to live in a foreign country, Canada, and to get acquainted with its biggest city, Toronto. Vince loved both, and he loved that he helped transform Toronto into a basketball town.

After his rookie season, Vince started thinking of Toronto, and Canada, as his home. Not just a temporarily adopted city, but his true home. While he had been attending UNC he still regarded Daytona Beach, FL, as his home base, but after joining the Raptors and the eruption of Vinsanity he really began building a new life in Canada. It felt a little bittersweet to watch him grow up and settle elsewhere, but that's parenthood.

So, sometime after his rookie year, Vince really began to put down roots in Toronto. When he had started in the League he'd rented a condo close to the arena where the team played—interestingly, this was owned by NBA Hall-of-Famer and former Toronto Raptor executive Isaiah Thomas; the NBA is a small world—but after Vince's rookie season he wanted something more permanent that he could call his own. We started looking for a new, permanent home for him in Toronto. He wanted to find a place that was both part of a real neighborhood and also close to where the Raptors practiced and played their home games, at Scotiabank Arena. After viewing a variety of luxury residences, Vince found and purchased a beautiful penthouse on Queens Quay.

The Queens Quay neighborhood is located on the northern shoreline of downtown Toronto. In its industrial heyday, decades ago, it was part of a working wharf and port on Lake Ontario, where big ships docked and transferred freight to and from the city. The area hosted many large warehouses, docks and ferries to various ports of call, including Toronto Island across the bay.

Once heavy port activity began to decline in Queens Quay, developers began to build residential towers, restaurants and retail outlets along the shoreline. They eventually built both the Rogers Centre and Scotiabank Arena, two of Toronto's major sports venues, in the neighborhood too. After all, it was an easily accessible waterfront area that boasted beautiful views of the lake and its outer islands. Queens Quay became a very desirable, upscale neighborhood, and I fully approved of Vince making it his new home.

As mentioned, I also fell in love with Toronto and the surrounding cities. After a few years, as I began to spend more time there, it only made sense for me to purchase a condo there as well. So, I did—though it was more modest than a penthouse.

Vince and I both were officially part-time Canadians. I was, by that time, living in Toronto for most of the NBA season. I made it a point to attend every home game that I could. I didn't just root for my son though, I rooted for the

For the Record—What Happened in Toronto

whole team, with all my heart. As I said, I was friends with Raptor's #1 super fan Nav Bhatia, so I learned how to be a crazy passionate Raptors fan from the best.

I also became close with many other players on the team, and their families. I met great people like Antonio Davis, Muggsy Bogues, our cousin Tracy McGrady, and even Dell Curry and his family.

Dell played for the Raptors from 1999–2002, so he was there when Vince started with the team. I know my son learned some key basketball tips and strategy from Dell, who was about as savvy a veteran as they come. Dell's eldest son, Stephen Curry, was also part of that extended Raptors family back then. Steph was still a child, but he accompanied his dad to Raptors practices whenever he could. Vince spent many hours shooting hoops with young Steph and his brother Seth. I'm sure he gave both youngsters some pointers, too. Vince enjoyed mentoring kids whenever the chance presented itself. Steph and Seth basically grew up in the NBA world.

I also became friendly with many people associated with the Raptors franchise, and, of course, its fans. Vince and I felt so welcomed by everyone we met and energized by every positive fan encounter we had. Vince felt fully committed to both his new city and his team. We felt like family.

The team itself, however, was still a work in progress. The year prior to Vince's arrival (1997–98), the team won only 16 games. The NBA season is 82 games long, so this wasn't ideal, to put it mildly. Vince knew that a lot of work was needed for the team to get better, but he was up for the challenge.

Vince was accustomed to playing on winning basketball teams. Mainland High School, back in Daytona Beach, made the state Final Four his junior year and won the title his senior year. At the University of North Carolina, Vince and the Tar Heels made it to the NCAA Tournament Final Four in both his sophomore and his junior year. Vince played a major role in all those teams. Even the most gifted athlete does not, however, make it to these levels without putting in the work.

Vince would never have won NBA Rookie-of-the-Year if he hadn't put in the work. Vinsanity never would have happened if he hadn't put in the work. In fact, Vince's early season stats with the Raptors are a testimony to his work ethic. As mentioned, during his rookie season, even without the benefit of a full training camp and pre-season, he averaged 18.3 points per game (while playing 35 minutes per game). Those are great numbers for any NBA player, much less a rookie.

But during his second season, while playing only three more minutes per game, Vince elevated his output to 25.7 points per game, while improving just about every other aspect of his game. These were All-Star numbers, and the fans knew it, as Vince was voted as an All-Star during his second season. He never looked back. During that second season, Vince improved his 3-point percentage, free-throw percentage, defense, and more. You simply can't improve this much without working your butt off and being totally dedicated to winning. Vince did what it took.

I've said it before, that as a sports parent I've sometimes had it easy because I never had to push Vince too hard. He has always been self-disciplined, hardworking, and easygoing. It's a winning combination for anyone, and great to observe in your children. No matter how big Vince's accolades, achievements and fame became, he was never a prima donna, and he rarely complained about anything. Even his teammates marveled at what a regular guy he was. He never had an attitude or expected anybody to worship him. He only expected people to respect him and expect the best from him.

One of the most satisfying things to me about Vince's entire basketball career was how he readily adapted to every basketball level, without question or complaint. How he simply willed himself to be better and rose to every challenge on his own terms. He gave everything, while making it seem as easy as if it was predestined. But it wasn't easy; his success was the result of hard work, dedication, an obsession to improve, and the desire to win.

But just like in his winning high school and college days, he needed a solid team playing with him to go the distance. Vince wasn't happy just making the playoffs with Toronto; he wanted an NBA title. He knew the team needed upgrades at multiple positions, but they mostly needed another star player.

At first, he thought that "other" star player might be our cousin, Tracy McGrady. Even though Tracy had started at the Raptors a year before Vince, he didn't come into his own as a player until the next season. For whatever reason, the Raptors hadn't played Tracy much during his rookie season. Sometimes NBA teams are so stacked with veteran talent that rookies receive very little playing time. Usually, these teams are in contention for a championship, and coaches know it's rare for rookies to contribute during the playoffs. That 1997–98 Raptors team, however, was not in contention. As mentioned, the team had won very few games that season, so it was truly perplexing to me and Vince that Tracy had gotten so little playing time. Fortunately for Tracy (and ultimately Vince) the team's head coach had resigned late in the season, which was when the new head coach Butch Carter had taken over.

Tracy thrived under Coach Butch Carter, as did Vince. The first year that the two cousins played together, Tracy still came off the bench, but the quality of his play rose significantly, and he was scoring over 9 points a game. The next year was Tracy's breakout year, where he eventually became a starter and scored 15.4 points per game, while grabbing 6.3 rebounds. He was morphing into an All-Star before our very eyes. Vince and Tracy loved playing together; you couldn't miss their joy if you watched them in person. They challenged each other to be better, to excel, and to win. Which they did.

By the end of the 2000 season, teams could tell that Tracy was going to be special. As a budding star who had just become a free agent, he was also going to get paid. Although Tracy loved playing with Vince, he also dreamed of becoming "the guy" on a team, as Vince had become on the Raptors. The Orlando Magic wanted Tracy to be their "guy" and were willing to pay him a maximum contract. They worked out a sign-and-trade deal with the Raptors, which is a fancy way of saying that he was eventually traded to the Magic, who offered him an impressive $92 million, multi-year contract.

With Tracy leaving, on his own quest to be "the guy" on the Orlando Magic, the Raptors were in need of another star player. After all, even the great Michael Jordan played along with another Hall-of-Fame great, Scottie Pippen, when winning six NBA titles. The Bulls did a great job of building a cast around their most valuable player. Vince and Team Carter felt that Vince needed a similar-level squad.

Vince wanted to win an NBA championship so badly! When you have talents like Vince, there is no other goal. Vince knew he had the skills to lead a contending team, but again, he couldn't do it all by himself. Both Vince and Team Carter frequently lobbied the Raptors' management about improving the team. They, in turn, made promises to Team Carter that they understood the importance of acquiring another star—but this was more easily said than achieved.

For the 2001–02 season the Raptors did acquire Hakeem Olajuwon, in a trade with the Houston Rockets, which seemed promising at first. Hakeem is one of the all-time basketball greats, but unfortunately, by the fall of 2001, he was at the end of his career. Hakeem played a total of five games for Toronto, then promptly retired because of persistent back injuries. After 17 seasons playing in Houston, and winning two NBA championships, it was a very anti-climactic end to an otherwise stellar career for him. It also didn't solve the Raptors' talent gap.

That same season, after three years in the NBA, the injury bug finally hit Vince, too. He was suffering from patellar tendinitis, to the point that he could no longer play at his best. On March 26th, 2002, Vince had left knee surgery. At age 25, this was his first major surgery in his career. After the surgery, all was seemingly going well, when I got a call from Vince explaining to me that he was concerned because his knee had swollen to the point that it was unrecognizable. Vince's head coach at the time, the usually very mild-mannered Lenny Wilkins, started swearing out loud upon seeing Vince's knee, exclaiming, "It doesn't even look like a knee any more!" That is when I booked an appointment for Vince with the well respected surgeon Dr. James Andrews.

Dr. Andrews was one of the best sports surgeons in the world, and elite pro athletes from many different sports sought out his advice. Vince's all-day evaluation with him went well. Dr. Andrews' final recommendation was that the patient be given adequate time to heal and not rush into rehab or other physical activity. Vince was shut down for the season.

Now while playing for the Toronto Raptors in 2000–04, Vince led the field in votes for the NBA All-Star selection for the entire League. Yet in 2002, even though he garnered the most votes, Vince was not available to play in the All-Star game due to his injury. It must have been tough for my son to watch the game knowing that he had received the most votes and that so many fans wanted to see him in action. Adding a little insult to his injury, the Eastern Conference team was led in scoring by none other than Tracy McGrady, who scored 24 points. Although Tracy was still family, now that he and Vince were on different teams they were rivals.

Often athletes are their own worst enemy. Usually, they want to return to the court or field prior to completely healing from an injury. Their relationship with training staff is usually good, and athletes have a way of convincing them that they are physically fit. They want to get back in the game. During this period of rehab, Vince knew that his team needed him. After all, he was the leading scorer and was sure to sell tickets, too, with his high-flying act on the court. But we had to be patient. It was tough.

After a setback in the healing and rehab process, Vince finally returned to the court the following season. The Raptors were playing the best basketball that the franchise had ever experienced. The expectations of the fans and the organization was that the team would go deep into the post-season. They expected this because they believed in Vince Carter.

Canada had recently lost its other NBA franchise, the Vancouver Grizzlies, because in six NBA seasons the team never came close to having a winning record and was near last in the League in attendance. The team was also losing tens of millions of dollars each year. The NBA allowed the Grizzlies' team owner to sell the franchise to a businessman who relocated them to Memphis, Tennessee, back in the United States. Suddenly, at the start of the 2001–02 season, Canada only had one NBA team—Vince's Raptors. Nav told me it was also a wakeup call to Raptors fans about what could happen if your team wasn't very good. The Raptors fans were even more behind Vince now, and so was the entire country of Canada.

This put even more pressure on Vince to get back on the court and win. Fans started referring to the Raptors as "the house that Vince built" because his stardom and flashy success had helped put the team on the map. At the start of the 2002–03 season, Vince was back on top form—until he wasn't. This time, it was an ankle injury. Vince ended up only playing 43 games that season, or roughly half a season. Instead of going deep into the playoffs, the Raptors missed the post-season: only by 3 games, but Vince was heartbroken.

When expectations were disappointed, Vince fell back on the fact that he was playing with a group of capable guys, but a little more help was still needed. Vince had exploded onto the NBA scene, so there weren't very many ballers that did not want to play with him. There were times when Vince recommended top players to team management. These players, in addition to having a skill set that would blend well with Vince's game, had contracts that were a good fit for a trade, or free agency signing. In other words, Vince only recommended complementary players who were obtainable and would help build a winning culture. Yet none of the possibilities came to fruition. Despite their many promises, the Raptors managers did not deliver another star to the team while Vince was there.

The team's win record suffered as a result of management's disinterest in adding another star. Any time Vince or other key players were out with injuries, there was no one else to carry the team. This became frustrating for Team Carter and fans, and after three solid winning seasons with Vince, the 2002–03 Raptors finished second to last in the Eastern Conference. This was soul-crushing for Vince. Nav Bhatia took it pretty hard too and told me he had no idea what the team was doing, or even thinking. Everyone knew they needed more talent. But the only major move the team made was to fire general manager Glen Grunwald after the 2003–04 season ended.

When the general manager position became available, Team Carter was hopeful that Julius Erving, more famously known as "Dr. J," would be interviewed for the position, as he had recently been part of a successful Orlando Magic front office; but he was not.

There are those who believe that Vince became disgruntled when the Raptors organization did not show Julius Erving the courtesy of bringing him to the front office to be interviewed for the vacant general manager position. Yes, Vince Carter and thousands of others thought it disappointing that Julius "Dr. J." Erving was not, at minimum, shown the respect he deserved. But this was hardly the biggest of

Vince's concerns. It was difficult for us to understand what management wanted at this point. It was increasingly clear, however, that they weren't interested in building a powerhouse team around Vince.

Even though Vince loved being a Raptor and loved his new home city of Toronto with all his heart, he became so frustrated that he began to think about leaving. He wanted to be part of a contender. Vince never wanted to leave the Raptors. But after years of futility trying to get management to upgrade the team to contender level, Vince's management team had to have "that" conversation with him.

Somewhere in all of this, people got their tidy-whities in a wad about me having a parking space in the arena. My condo was two blocks from the Air Canada Centre. At first, I enjoyed walking to the games and riding home with Vince. On those crazy cold evenings, I would go to the ACC early and have dinner. I was always invited to stop by the Director's Lounge for fellowship and a little libation. But then, on a few of the walks to the arena, strange things happened. Once, a loud blaring marriage proposal came my way by a cab driver. I was confused, and relieved when a couple of nice young gentlemen escorted me into the arena, safely away from the commotion. Then there was the occasion when I decided to drive to the game and parked in the lot across from the Air Canada Centre. A few feet from my vehicle, I was mobbed by adoring fans who wanted my autograph and to take photos. I eventually managed to make my way safely across the street, but I was shaken. I knew the fans meant well, but I wasn't used to the attention, like Vince was, so I panicked a little. Then, there was the time when there was a protest just outside of the arena, and the protestors had traffic backed up for what seemed to be miles. Other stuck fans and I were not happy about this. We missed the tip-off. Meanwhile, Vince knew that I should have been in my seat long before the national anthem. Vince sent a posse to look for me; they heard about the protest,

A Basketball Mom's Memoir

The "Three Musketeers," Vince Carter, Ademola Okulaja, and Antawn Jamison, in 1994, with the Atlantic Coast Conference (ACC) championship trophy. (Courtesy of UNC Athletics)

Vince Carter with the 1994 ACC championship trophy, when the University of North Carolina defeated Virginia 73–66. (Courtesy of UNC Athletics)

The Making of Vince Carter

Vince Carter, dunking in the Dean E. Smith Center, University of North Carolina, 1997. (Courtesy of UNC Athletics)

A Basketball Mom's Memoir

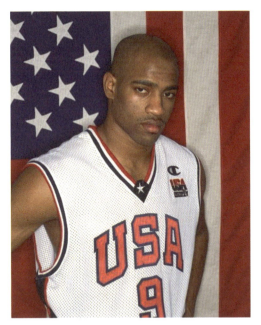

Vince Carter representing the United States in the 2000 Olympics when the US Basketball team won Gold. (Courtesy of USA Basketball)

Caption USA Junior Team 1994. Vincent Carter, no. 7, is kneeling, third from right. (Courtesy of USA Basketball)

The Making of Vince Carter

It has been coined "the Dunk of Death." (Above) Vince Carter was cleared for take-off over Frenchman Frederic Weis in the 2000 Olympic Games in Australia. (Right) The moment after this incredible feat. The US Basketball Team went on to win Gold. (Courtesy of USA Basketball)

A Basketball Mom's Memoir

Vincent Carter and his mom Michelle Carter chat prior to the University of North Carolina Commencement on the morning of May 20th, 2001. (Carter family collection)

Stuart Scott, ESPN Sportscaster, Anchor, and 1987 UNC graduate (pictured with Vincent) was the UNC Spring 2001 Commencement speaker on the occasion of Vince's graduation. (Courtesy of ESPN)

The Making of Vince Carter

Vince Carter is an eight-time NBA All-Star. (Courtesy of NBA)

Vince prepares for his duty as the 2009 Coke 400 pace car driver. (Courtesy of NASCAR)

A Basketball Mom's Memoir

Fan posters for Vince Carter as a Dallas Maverick.

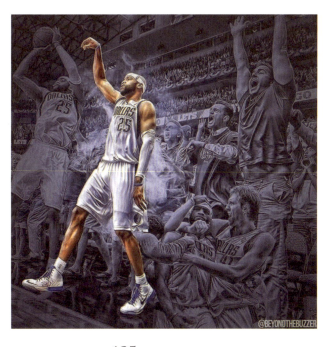

Vince Carter shoots the basketball for the Atlanta Hawks, 2018. (Courtesy of Atlanta Hawks)

Vince Carter bids farewell to the fans on March 11th, 2020. NBA games came to a halt over COVID concerns. This Atlanta Hawks overtime loss to the New York Knicks was Vince's last NBA game. (Courtesy of Atlanta Hawks Basketball)

and they guessed—accurately—that I was caught in the melee. It was after these occurrences that I was offered an underground parking space in the arena for home games. I gracefully and thankfully accepted, but somehow local media found out about my parking space and made it into a divisive issue. They actually tried to shame me for wanting to feel safe. A reserved parking space wasn't exactly the height of luxury, just for my security. I thought it strange anyone would make this into an issue.

Also on the "I'm mad at Vince list" was his participation in his college graduation. Vince and I had an agreement that, at an appropriate time in his career, he would return to UNC to complete the requirements for his bachelor's degree, as he had promised aged 18. Possibly in some families education is not a big deal but in ours it is and always has been. The term "student-athlete" meant just that. You are a student first. After going pro, Vince diligently attended summer school for three terms at UNC—after he became a solid millionaire. Once all academic requirements were completed, he was eligible to order his cap and gown, and pay for his campus parking tickets. I was not ready for the latter, but it is what it is.

Our family was extremely proud of the commitment Vince made. A man in his position could have spent his summers engaged in more glamorous activities and lavish vacations. Instead, Vince put receiving his college degree at the top of his "to do" list and kept his promise to me. May 20th, 2001, was one of the most precious days of my life. My eldest child received his bachelor's degree, and I was there to see him enter Kenan Stadium adorned in his Carolina Blue cap and gown, amongst all the other graduates and academicians.

Meanwhile, on the career front, there were matters to resolve. We had tried our best to build a winning culture in Toronto. Vince had surely done his part, so why wasn't his commitment returned? Team Carter, in good faith, held several meetings with the Raptors' ownership, general manager and president. There were promises made that were not fulfilled. One was to get Vince more help on the court. Year after year, however, that promise was not kept. In a career, just as in a marriage, when promises go unfulfilled, the relationship has failed.

11

Going for Olympic Gold

The year 2000 was the start of a new millennium and a great time for basketball. For Vince, spring 2000 represented his second year as a professional basketball player and his first season leading the Raptors to the playoffs. His stats in that second season rose dramatically, to the point that he was not just the leading scorer on the Raptors but also the fourth highest in points per game in the entire NBA. With his high-flying and dunking appearances at the 1999 and 2000 All-Star game and dunk contest, he had already made a name for himself in the NBA and among fans. Vinsanity had begun and swept across Canada, the United States and other parts of the world.

    The year 2000 was also the year the Olympiad was held in Sydney, Australia. This was the third time that professional basketball had been represented. Before 1992, the Olympics had only been open to amateur athletes (though some countries had found ways to circumvent this rule). Then, in the late 1980s, the International Olympic Committee had finally amended their rules to allow pro athletes in a range of sports, including basketball, to compete. This change was great for the sport, as it enabled the best basketball to be showcased globally.

In 1992, Michael Jordan led the original basketball Olympic Dream Team for the United States. Before this, Team USA had mostly consisted of elite college players who did their best to represent their country on the world stage. If the Olympic Committee had never changed the rules, I like to think that Team USA would one day have approached college student Vince with an offer to play on the team. I believe he would have thrived in such an environment—we will never know. We almost didn't know in 2000 whether pro Vince would compete on the team.

Originally, Vince was not selected to play on the 2000 USA Olympic Basketball Team. Again, this was his second, breakout, year in the NBA, and he was the leader in the NBA All-Star voting that season. It was confusing to me that he wasn't initially invited. There was a precedent for USA Basketball to select a young up-and-coming star player to participate. The previous USA Olympic Team had included Grant Hill, who was 23 years old when he joined Team USA. Like Vince, Hill had been in his second season in the NBA when invited to be part of the team.

Hill, who had played the small forward position for the Detroit Pistons, had posted an incredible stat-line during his sophomore season, too. He was scoring over 20 points, and pulling down nearly 10 rebounds, per game. He had also led the nation in All-Star votes. It was a no brainer for Team USA to make Grant Hill part of the team in 1996.

During his second season, Vince wowed fans all over the world. I remember being not only disappointed that Vince was passed over for the team but also perplexed. What did my son need to do to make the team?

The 2000 Team USA was stacked with veteran talent, including Alonzo Mourning, Jason Kidd, Gary Payton, Tim Hardaway, and Allan Houston, just to name a few. Those guys had earned their starting minutes and leadership roles on the team. Vince's former teammate from his AAU days, Kevin Garnett, was also selected. Kevin was just a year older than Vince, but in 1997 he had gone straight to the NBA out of high school without attending college. Therefore, in 2000, he was much more established in the League than Vince. He was already regarded as the franchise player, or "the guy" for the Minnesota Timberwolves at that time.

The Team USA roster was initially set in January 2000. In March 2000, however, Tom Gugliotta of the Phoenix Suns withdrew due to a serious knee injury that required reconstructive surgery. (Fortunately, Gugliotta would fully recover from the injury, but not before a lengthy rehab process.) It was then that Vince was invited to join Team USA.

I was excited and proud that Vince had the amazing honor to represent the United States of America doing something that he loved—playing basketball. I felt honored just to be a part of the USA Basketball traveling party. It just didn't get any better than being with the Olympic team for six weeks, in beautiful hotels, dining in fine restaurants, watching basketball, and doing a little shopping along the way. Attending or participating in an Olympics is an awesome bucket-list experience. But the trip would end up being somewhat more taxing than my initial vision of paradise.

Prior to the actual 2000 Olympics, there was what we called "the Tour." Before Team USA flew to Sydney for the games, the team played what I called tune-up "friendly" games in Maui, Hawaii; Tokyo, Japan; and, finally, Melbourne, Australia. The tune-up Tour lasted approximately four weeks and involved a great deal of globe-trotting across the Pacific Ocean. Although these games were played against international teams, the wins didn't count towards national or Olympic standings; but even though the games were called "friendlies," they were anything but.

Melbourne, Australia, was where Team USA played the last of its tune-up friendlies before the Olympics. These competitions against the Australian national team were the fiercest, and there were moments when things got downright nasty. My son Vince Carter and Australian Andrew Gage seemed to get under each other's skin. "Umm, Vince! Look around. We are in Australia!" is what I might have said but didn't. The headlines over the next few days referred to Vince in unfriendly—in fact, insulting—terms. Well, so much for the "friendly."

Not only were these last games intense, but so was the environment in Melbourne, at least to this visiting American. There were protests occurring throughout Melbourne involving some anti-capitalist and anti-Western, including anti-American, sentiment. I'm not much of a political person—I don't have the stomach for it—so I'm not sure if I even understood the politics of this protest back then. Now, I don't recall what it was all about. But I remember the city was also hosting a summit where major politicians from around the world were meeting to discuss various issues. The protests were directed more towards that event than Team USA Basketball. But some of the protest spilled over and I remember glimpsing a little of it.

The USA Basketball traveling party lodged at a luxury hotel on the waterfront in downtown Melbourne. Because of the protest, we had heightened security at the hotel. Protestors had been harassing some of the members of the USA women's basketball team as they took water-taxis to and from the hotel to practice. I'll never forget watching, from the hotel room window, some protestors on a bridge throw stuff onto the water-taxis below. I don't believe the protestors hurt anyone, but it was still wrong of them to be harassing the athletes, who had nothing to do with world politics or the summit meeting. I was staying on the 25th or so floor of the hotel so I had quite the view. I remember voicing my concern for the safety of our players to the USA Basketball staff. I was relieved when they agreed with me and informed me that they had already cancelled that day's practice and subsequent activities.

One day, we also experienced a total lockdown while at the hotel in Melbourne, where security ordered the players and everyone else to stay in the hotel all day because of a security risk. After totally peaceful trips to Hawaii and Japan, this was both unexpected and a little frightening. But we made the best of it and without incident continued our journey to Sydney.

Team USA was coached by Hall-of-Fame coach Rudy Tomjanovich, who had led the Houston Rockets to win two back-to-back NBA championships, in 1993 and 1994. In Hawaii, Coach Tomjanovich had focused on getting the Team USA players acclimated to one another's playing style and on developing a team strategy for the Olympic Games. The team, after all, hadn't had much time or opportunity to practice together. Its opponents throughout the friendlies, on the other hand, were mainly veteran national or professional teams composed of players who were very used to each other's game. These teams were of course focused on doing anything they could to defeat the United States and viewed the friendlies as a once-in-a-lifetime chance to play against, and maybe even beat, the best NBA players and best basketball team in the world. So the competitors played their hearts out, and the on-court action was fierce. I was glad when the friendlies ended because I felt that Vince and his teammates needed to save their energies for the upcoming games in Australia, the ones that counted towards a medal.

The players, coaches, and players' families were all traveling together on the same team jet airplane and staying in the same hotels. We were like one big Olympic family. I got to know some of the other players and their kin quite well. I recall learning that Vin Baker, who at the time played center for the Seattle Supersonics, was an excellent chef. Most of the suites in the hotels where we lodged had kitchens, which helped the players maintain their strict (or not so strict) diets. Vin sometimes cooked meals for the team and their families. Let me tell you, they were delicious; and the home-style cooking was welcomed. Vin was serious about his cooking. The time I spent with my extended family for these six weeks was much appreciated, as it kept me from dwelling on personal issues.

Despite all of the glory of the Olympics, this was also a personally tense time for my family. For one: Vince had hair! Normally, hair is not an issue. But when you have flaunted the bald head since high school, like Vince did, a change gets noticed. I think his sudden head of hair was a signal to me that things were getting heavy for him. In the months prior to the Olympics, Vince lost a significant legal battle with the sportswear company Puma. His agent, William "Tank" Black, was dealing with very public legal troubles. Meanwhile, I was in the midst of a divorce. I believed that the growing of the hair was because, at that time, Vince Carter did not want to be Vince Carter. But he did his best to work through his troubles.

Vince took his preparations for the Games extremely seriously. I remember he didn't want to do much other than practice, play and think about basketball. My birthday happened during the actual Olympic Games, but, other than taking me out to buy me a gift of a designer handbag, Vince was all business. Normally, because my birthday occurred before the NBA season began, my son made the day extra special for me. But not Olympic Vince. He was so intense in his training that he did little else. I think he fully understood the gravitas of his situation: that he was among the best players on planet earth, and he therefore wanted to be his absolute best. On the evening before my birthday, the players went out to have a night of fun, as they had a rest day the following day. Of course, family and friends who were in Sydney were welcome to join as well; but not even my upcoming birthday could get my son out. He stayed at the hotel.

The Olympic Games last for 16 days. Along with the competitions in approximately 35 sports, there are magnificent opening and closing ceremonies. The opening ceremony was on September 15th, 2000, and it was jaw-dropping—magnificent. There was a tremendous amount of buzz around who would light the Olympic cauldron. The identity of this person is always top secret.

As it happened, I had begun to read and hear many conversations about the Aboriginal people in Australia. I hadn't previously known anything about them, but I learned that they had been treated poorly over the years. I found it interesting that the Aboriginal Australians had skin color like African Americans. The plight of these people piqued my interest. I was so intrigued that I attended a live theatrical performance about the Aboriginal people at the famed Sydney Opera House. Little did I realize that this new interest of mine would prove relevant to the Olympics.

The Olympic opening ceremony lasted four and a half hours and was viewed by billions of people worldwide. It was so exciting to be a part of it, even in the stands. Then the moment was upon us. Who would light the Olympic cauldron? Rising from a breathtaking display of water, lights and flames, appeared the Aboriginal 400-meter sprinter Cathy Freeman. The gasps from over 100,000 spectators in the stands were deafening.

The next day, September 16th, 2000, the competitions began. The first five men's basketball games were played every other day, starting with the September 17th matchup against China, which the USA won. The second game was against Italy on September 19th. I was so proud to watch Vince lead the USA in scoring in this game, with 13 points, as the USA cruised to win 93–61. Any Olympic jitters Vince had were gone. Four days later, Vince once again led Team USA in scoring, with 18 points in a victory against New Zealand.

On September 25th, when the USA played France, Vince performed one of those dunks that, I believe, will be talked about until the end of sporting history. The victim of this athletic wonderment was a 7'2" Frenchman, Frederic Weiss, who a year previously had been drafted for the New York Knicks but returned to France without signing his rookie contract, crediting it to hostility from fans. In the USA–France game, Vince, while driving to the basket, dunked over Weiss, all seven feet and two inches of him. Vince achieved this by getting a running start, leaping, then placing one hand on Weiss's shoulder and using Weiss as support to propel himself up further and slam the basket home. Vince cleanly dunked over the gigantic Weiss! The crowd didn't go wild at first—they were too shocked. This really was a moment of awe when no one even knew what to say, including me.

Then, as the dunk replay was shown and the crowd got proof they really had witnessed this unprecedented dunk, the fans went wild. Vince's teammates—both on the floor and on the sidelines—went wild also. Even the French media did: they respected what they saw, naming it the *le Dunk de la Mort* (the Dunk of Death), which is still used to this day. I believe this is the only in-game dunk over a seven-foot player in history. Certainly it is at the Olympics.

After the win against France, the "sudden death" medal round began. Eight teams qualified for this round to determine who would win Bronze, Silver, and Gold.

Team USA faced Russia first, in the quarterfinals, then Lithuania in the semis and finally France, again, in the Gold Medal final game. Unlike in the earlier qualifying round, where the games were spaced two days apart, the first two medal games were held one day after another, on September 28th and 29th, meaning there were no rest days in between these critical games.

The USA did not breeze through the medial rounds. France, Lithuania, and Russia all gave us several anxious moments. But Vince was, again, the high scorer for Team USA against Lithuania in the semifinal, with 18 points. Finally, the championship game, to determine who won the Gold, was held between the USA and, again, France on October 1st. After what Vince did to France in the qualifying round, a lot of fans were eager for the re-match, including me. Vince didn't leap over Weiss again, but, crucially, he scored 13 points and tied with Alan Houston who also scored 13, as Team USA's top scorers. This was enough to secure for Team USA their dream result—their Gold Medal win!

When the medals were awarded, it was Gold–USA, Silver–France, and Bronze–Lithuania. Vince and his team were now officially the best in the world. Vince led the USA Basketball Team on points and was third overall in the 2000 Olympics basketball scoring, with 14.8 points per game. I was so proud to be able to think: Vince Carter, once an Olympian, always an Olympian!

The closing ceremony for the Games of the XXVII Olympiad was held that same day, October 1st, 2000. USA Basketball and its traveling party did not attend though, as the Olympics had gone on late into the summer and NBA training camps were about to start. Some players weren't allowed any time off by their NBA teams and had to report directly from the Olympics to training camp! That was a lot to expect, and it was disappointing for players to miss the closing ceremony.

NBA training camps started on October 3rd. For Vince and me, the flight from Sydney to Atlanta, GA, was approximately 21 hours, including a couple of layovers. From Atlanta, Vince would continue on to Toronto while I flew into Daytona Beach, Florida. Vince was excused from training camp for a couple of days. Team USA Basketball players and the USA traveling party were exhausted. The physical and emotional drain was overwhelming at times. But of course, it was all worth it.

Fortunately, Vince was given a short rest period after the 2000 Olympic victory before he rejoined his Raptors teammates in camp. This was the same year that Vince sustained his first major injury in the NBA. Possibly, going from one NBA season to the Olympics, and to the next NBA season took a physical toll.

12

From Canada to the Peach State (and Places in Between)

One of the things that's most remarkable about my son is how long he played professional basketball at the highest level. To date, he holds the record for the longest NBA career—22 seasons. I hope I've imparted some of the secrets of his success in this book. It was quite a remarkable ride.

Vince Carter played for a total of eight NBA teams: Toronto Raptors, New Jersey Nets (now the Brooklyn Nets), Orlando Magic, Phoenix Suns, Dallas Mavericks, Memphis Grizzlies, Sacramento Kings, and Atlanta Hawks. Uniquely for a player in the NBA, his 22-year career spanned four different decades—1990s, 2000s, 2010s, and 2020s. He retired at the end of the 2020 NBA season.

Vince started his NBA career with a rather steeper cultural learning curve than other players who were drafted by teams in the United States. At the start of his pro career in Toronto, he had little to go on regarding life in the city. After learning the Raptors' playbook, the location of the home team locker room, where the team practices, and the names of the coaches and trainers, he was eager to learn about the culture of Canada, which was of course an entirely new country for him. Though there are many similarities between how Americans and Canadians live, there are also vast differences. At each NBA game, the United States and Canadian national anthems are performed. To show respect, our family thought it was important to learn the words of the Canadian anthem and embrace what we could to fit in. With the Raptors, Vince was fortunate to wear his longtime preferred jersey number, 15.

To this day, Vince often pays homage to Charles Oakley, Dell Curry, Dee Brown, Mark Jackson, Muggsy Bogues, Alvin Williams, Hayward Workman, Antonio Davis, and Kevin Willis. These were the Toronto Raptors veterans who took Vince under their wing. Later, with the New Jersey Nets, Vince was like a kid in a candy store as he was excited to play with one of the best point guards in the game, Jason Kidd. While on the Nets, Vince also played with All-Star veteran forward Richard Jefferson, another great. Jefferson and Vince created headaches for opposing defenses. Vince learned a ton from the veterans who helped him along the way. Vince says, "Today locker rooms are flipped. There may be two or three veterans and ten or eleven players with less than four years of experience." Vince was happy he had the opportunity to absorb so much wisdom from the veteran-heavy teams he played on.

Though Vince was constantly being compared with Michael Jordan, especially at the start of his career, he sought out to be the best Vince Carter that he could be. Vince always admired and respected Michael Jordan for his athletic ability, and appreciated the fact that they were both University of North Carolina alums and both played the shooting guard position. These were the similarities. But Vince also understood that God made each individual unique. He embraced and appreciated his own uniqueness. Therefore, he never wanted to be like someone else, he just wanted to achieve greatness on his own terms.

While playing with the Toronto Raptors, Vince sustained the worst injury that he ever had. The lingering knee injury required him to have surgery. According to the medical doctors, the surgery and his recovery went well. Yet, I observed that afterwards Vince never seemed to be quite physically the same. As he continued to play, occasionally his surgically repaired knee would swell, and he complained about Achilles pain too. But Vince loves to play basketball, so he played through the pain. Most NBA greats play through pain for at least part of their careers. It's how it's always been.

In Toronto, most of the burden of winning was placed on Vince's shoulders. So, after his knee injury, it was imperative for the Raptors to add big-time talent, in order to truly compete for a championship. Because Vince was playing outstanding basketball, many players throughout the NBA expressed an interest in playing with him. On several occasions, Vince would make recommendations to the Raptors' general manager, Glen Grunwald. If Glen thought that the player could help the team and was a good fit, he would pass the recommendation on to those who made the final decision. Over the six years that Vince was with the Raptors, none of the recommendations came to fruition. Between 1998 and 2004, Vince had three different coaches: Butch Carter, Lenny Wilkens, and Kevin O'Neill. While learning to embrace the nuances of different coaches, Vince tried to help the team advance farther than they had the previous season.

It has been well publicized that there was a contentious parting of ways between Vince and the Raptors. Many of the comments we read and heard about this were outlandish. It was my advice to Vince not to get caught up in the back and forth of responding. I believed that the truth would eventually come to light. It always does.

For approximately six years after Vince left the Raptors, I sat through the most horrid, nasty, booing and the meanest comments I had ever experienced, whenever Vince returned to Toronto to play the Raptors. There never seemed to be any animosity towards Vince by the Raptors players; the venom came from fans—not all, but many. I don't think these fans realized what had really happened. As the years went on, more of the truth was revealed from various sources. The booing became less and less, and the understanding of how Vince had transformed the organization became clearer.

In 2014, the Toronto Raptors organization honored Vince with a wonderful video tribute. Most of the fans in the sold-out arena gave Vince a standing ovation, led by our good friend Nav Batia. Neither Vince nor I knew that he would be honored that night. It was a pleasant and emotional surprise. I am very grateful to have been there to see the crowd and hear the well deserved respect for what Vince brought to Canada.

Vince and I love Toronto. It was unfortunate that the ending of his time there was not more positive. Aside from the basketball games, Vince and I miss hosting our summer youth basketball camps, reading to children in various locations in the greater Toronto area, hosting Christmas parties for the children living in hostels, and just being out and about in Toronto. But all that came to an end when Vince was finally traded.

On December 17th, 2004, Vince was traded to the New Jersey Nets for Alonzo Mourning, Aaron Williams, Eric Williams, and two first-round draft picks. Alonzo Mourning never reported to the Raptors to play. There was a contract buyout that would release Zo from the Raptors. Several media outlets called this trade the most lopsided deal in NBA history, meaning the Raptors made the worst trade in NBA history because the team got so little in return for Vince.

When an NBA player is traded during the season, he has 48 hours to report to his new team. Those 48 hours are extremely hectic, and the logistics of relocating in such a short period of time are a nightmare. Being traded a week prior to Christmas made the logistics even more daunting. Usually, players leave their families behind while they get settled in their new city, secure transportation, and find a place to live. All this happens while there are games being played and new teammates to get accustomed to, and a new playbook to learn. There must be someone who is the glue, the boots-on-the-ground person, to hold everything together. In Vince's case, that was me. Vince's agent handled the trade. My role was to make sure the other items on the checklist were actually checked.

When Vince was traded to the Nets, it was an especially arduous time for the Carter family. Aside from Vince needing to get to New Jersey, his personal assistant, Jeff Scott, had to relocate as well. In addition, Vince's then wife, Ellen, had just surpassed the first trimester of her pregnancy. That meant new medical professionals would have to be sought out. After a short time in Weehawken, Vince and his family finally settled in a beautiful home in Saddle River, New Jersey.

It was a joy to be a part of the New Jersey Nets family. The Nets organization had one of the most helpful Basketball Operations Departments of all the teams Vince played with. From a distance, I watched how Coach Lawrence Frank managed the team. It was masterful. It's worth noting that later, in 2016, Coach Frank was hired as the President of Basketball Operations for the Los Angeles Clippers, and that in 2020 he would be honored by the NBA as Executive-of-the-Year. I saw from day one how good he was.

Vince truly enjoyed playing with his Nets teammates. He lived very close to Jason Kidd and his family. This gave Vince opportunities to pick his brain—Jason is one of the top all-time NBA point guards.

When I went to New Jersey to visit, Jason and his family made me feel welcome. Everyone associated with the team was very friendly. As we had done in Toronto, I continued to organize summer youth basketball camps hosted by Vince. Several of his teammates would make appearances and work on basketball skills with the campers. That basketball family feeling was back. The New Jersey Nets team was very good. Vince experienced a great deal of success there.

Being traded is part of being a professional athlete in any sport. After five years with the New Jersey Nets (2004—09), Vince was traded home to play for coach Stan Van Gundy and the Orlando Magic. Basketball fans in Central Florida were thrilled that their native son was coming home. Orlando is approximately a one-hour drive from Daytona Beach and neighboring cities. There was a lot of excitement amongst Central Florida basketball fans and in the media. It was great for me. I did not miss a home game. Every game, I would see fans who had cheered for Vince throughout his basketball career, starting with his Mainland High School days.

Vince was celebrated in his hometown, too. Daytona Beach is the headquarters for the National Association for Stock Car Auto Racing NASCAR. In 2009, Vince accepted the honor to be the honorary pace-car driver for the Coke Zero 400 race. To Vince's surprise, the pace-car was a Chevrolet Camaro with a stick shift. Vince had never driven a stick shift vehicle in his life! The day prior to the race, NASCAR Sprint Cup Series official Buster Auton put on his driver's red cap and jumped in the passenger seat. Vince, at 6'6", folded his frame into the car. I stood on the sidelines thinking to myself, "Who learns how to drive a stick shift on the track of the Daytona 500!?" Vince admitted that he was nervous about his role as the pace-car driver, especially having to drive the stick shift. But he was determined to do it right. He told me, "This is the driver's Super Bowl. I have to keep the pace. I can't mess this up!"

According to Vince, Auton kept telling him, "It's OK, there's no pressure. Pretend you're shooting a 3-pointer with the game on the line." Thankfully, all went well. Vince kept the pace. He said he looked in the rear-view mirror and all he could see were headlights. The drivers were inches from the bumper of the pace-car. Vince said, "I just kept telling myself: I can't mess this up." I honestly think it was harder for Vince to keep pace leading the Daytona 500 than it was for him to dunk over a giant Frenchman in the Olympics or shoot a game-winning 3-pointer.

Compared with Vince's statistics with the Toronto Raptors and the New Jersey Nets, one might describe Vince's tenure with Orlando Magic as pedestrian—although he played in the Eastern Conference finals with the Magic. Overall, Vince's experience in Orlando was rewarding, and the team went far. The coaching of Stan Van Gundy helped Vince grow as an NBA athlete.

The trade to the Phoenix Suns in 2010 came out of nowhere. At least for me, it was not expected. This trade occurred on December 18th, 2010, when the Magic took part in a six-player trade that sent Vince west. Once again, Vince found himself having to get acclimated to a new team and location: this time, in the western United States—Arizona, which is about 2,000 miles from Central Florida. The challenges of finding Vince housing, transportation, and the like, all started again for me.

The Phoenix Suns were coached by Alvin Gentry, who was a solid coach, and Vince played well from the start—but there was a situation with the jersey number! Vince had worn jersey number 15 since he was in high school, but at Phoenix Suns his new teammate Robin Lopez already wore number 15 when Vince arrived, so the number was not available. Vince called me to explain the jersey dilemma. I could hear the anguish in his voice. This east coast guy is traded out of nowhere to the west coast. Now, his longtime jersey number is not available. What next? Vince and I discussed adding the 1 and 5 for jersey number 6, but Suns great Walter Davis had worn that number for the Suns, and it had been retired by the team. We thought about number 51, but that just seemed weird. So, for whatever reason, 25 was his choice. Vince has always realized that playing in the NBA was living a dream. Even though this period was not as he imagined his career would develop, he remained thankful. From my vantage point, Vince played with the idea of winning games, but I never felt this team was a great fit.

To add to the shock and awe, following the conclusion of the NBA lockout in December 2011, the Phoenix Suns waived Vince in a cost-cutting move. Vince was due to be paid $18 million for the upcoming 2011–12 season. By waiving him, the Suns would owe Vince the much smaller sum of $4 million.

This was after Vince came to the team in mid-season the previous year, playing in 51 games, starting 41 of those games, and averaging 13.5 points per game while shooting 42%. This paints a vivid picture of "it's a business." His salary was drastically decreased by a team to which he brought real value. But that didn't matter: the Suns used the unique league and contract situation to their advantage, and apparently didn't value the fact he made their team better.

In December 2011, Vince signed a three-year contract with the Dallas Mavericks. This was an exciting move for him. Again, jersey number 15 was retired. Therefore, it was his second round of wearing number 25. But, overall, things went well in Dallas. Coach Carlisle offered this assessment of Vince:

> I remember Vince Carter as an amazing physical talent coming out of UNC in the Spring of 1998. At that time, I was an assistant coach for the Indiana Pacers. It was at the end of my first year working as an assistant for Larry Bird. We had the 12th pick in the 1998 NBA Draft. So, I had a pretty good feel for the prospects that year. Vince was drafted by Toronto and began what was a highly anticipated NBA career. One of the very first Sports Center-type highlights came in a game early in Vince's rookie season against the Pacers. He drove the left baseline and went up like he was going to dunk the ball on the left side of

the basket—then brought it down below his waist, continued forward to the opposite side of the basket, brought it even lower, then WHAM!!—unbelievable reverse dunk. Easily the sickest dunk I had ever seen. I turned to Larry Bird sitting next to me on the bench. We looked at each other and simultaneously said, "Holy Shit".

Vince was a young superstar and perennial All-Star who had a great run in Toronto. Then a strong five years in New Jersey. Then two years in Orlando which was home for him. Then one year at Phoenix. At this point, it was uncertain what Vince had left. As you go from long successful runs in stable situations to shorter more transient stints with teams, people start questioning everything—off-court habits, commitment to conditioning, love of the game, etc. When we signed Vince to a mid-level exception deal with the Mavericks in December 2011, coming out of that summer's lockout, Vince's market value had dipped. We hoped that his game had not.

The colorful owner of the team, Mark Cuban, came as advertised. Fans could not help getting excited when they saw his intensity at games, as he sat in the stands among the fans. From a distance, I watched how Coach Rick Carlisle managed and taught the nuances of the NBA game. He was stellar! For Coach Carlisle to keep his poise when the animated boss Mark Cuban was sitting to his right practically every game was something special to me. I tip my hat to that team. All the action that sometimes occurred near their bench never seemed to be a distraction.

This was an exciting time for the Carter family. Vince was playing with Dirk Nowitzki and he was reunited with Jason Kidd. At this point in Vince's career, he had reinvented himself and changed his game. Having started out as a slasher, Vince had developed a reliable 3-point shot. Actually, he'd always had a reliable 3-point shot, but now he just used it a lot more. The slashing and dunking did not go away, but dunks became side dishes instead of the main shooting course. This also marked the beginning of Vince coming off of the bench in the role of the sixth man. As basketball players age, they are faced with a challenging decision: either adapt their game and stick around, or simply fade away. For players who were once superstars, this is a tough decision. Vince Carter is a realist and has what some may call "old folks" common sense. Here is the choice. Do you accept a less glamorous role and/or change your game to stay in the League? Accept or reject? Vince accepted it. According to Coach Carlisle:

> From day 1 of training camp of the 2011-12 season, Vince Carter was awesome. A great pro and teammate. He arrived early to practice and stayed late. He nurtured our young players and played his ass off. Vince started his first year with us and presented a nearly impossible post match-up for opponents at the 2-position. That year, his play lifted us to a playoff berth.
>
> The following year, Vince came to me with a request that truly set him apart. Jason Terry, who had been a top player for our championship team in 2011 and the best sixth man in the NBA, was not coming back for the 2012-13 season. When Vince found out about this, he asked that we meet. In the meeting, Vince asked if he could "have the honor of becoming our sixth man". He acknowledged how special Jason Terry's accomplishments were and saw the obvious void that was left. I was absolutely floored at Vince's offer. The way he approached it with the class and respect he showed Jason Terry was just tremendous. The next two years, he was an enormous part of our success.

At Dallas, midway through the first quarter, Dirk would come out of the game. His replacement was Vince. Vince embraced this sixth man role. He began to let his experience shine and played smarter. You could see the veteran savvy in every game. It was important to Coach Carlisle for Vince to be on the floor during crunch-time. When it mattered.

As a Maverick, Vince also found himself coaching younger players from the sidelines. This helped the Mavericks' second unit become one of the most efficient and effective offenses in the NBA.

Because winning is paramount to Vince, it seems that the transition from star starter to effective bench player was seamless. He wasn't revving it up as much as he used to, but he was still making the engine hum.

There was one game I'll never forget. It's April 26th, 2014, playoff time. The Dallas Mavericks were hosting the San Antonio Spurs for game 3. The series was tied 1–1. This was a huge game between the Texas rivals. The game was going back and forth. With two ticks of the clock remaining, the Spurs were up 108–106. The Mavs took the ball out from the left sideline. Monta Ellis ran off a curl towards the top of the key. Jose Calderon decided to pass the ball to Vince who broke towards the left corner with Manu Ginobili sprinting towards him. Somehow, Vince caught the pass from Calderon, turned towards the baseline in one motion, used a quick fake pump that got Ginobili in the air, and drained a fallaway 3-pointer. Mavs 109, Spurs 108—game over. The crowd went bonkers, and so did the Mavs team. In the midst of the mayhem was Mark Cuban celebrating along with his guys. Admittedly, I stopped breathing for those two seconds, but all is well that ends well. According to Coach Carlisle, "Vince hit one of the biggest shots in Dallas Mavericks franchise history—a playoff game-winning 3-pointer."

The media coverage that followed compared this shot with the fallaway 3-point attempt on May 20th, 2001, during the Eastern Conference Championship game against the Philadelphia Sixers, where Vince missed an eerily similar short while playing for the Toronto Raptors.

The 2013–14 season would be Vince's last in Dallas. Again, this is when the "business of the NBA" stings. Coach Carlisle summed things up this way:

> In the NBA change is a constant. The next several years, Vince would move on to Memphis, Sacramento and Atlanta. He continued to play at an amazing level into his late 30s and early 40s. Over a career spanning two-plus decades, Vince Carter set the bar extraordinarily high in so many ways. He was an eight-time All-Star and will be a first ballot Hall-of-Famer. He became one of the best sixth men ever to play in the NBA. He mentored countless young players, helping them develop their games and professionalism. He was, and remains, one of the greatest

ambassadors the game of basketball has ever seen. All this with great humility, dignity, and grace. I, personally, thank Vince for making my three years with him in Dallas three of the most memorable I have ever experienced in the NBA.

In July 2014, Vince signed a three-year deal with the Memphis Grizzlies. Memphis, here we come. Once again, I was tasked with situating Vince. I had it down to an art form by then. Memphis was, after all, Vince's sixth city.

When Vince arrived in Memphis, Dave Joerger was the head coach. In 2016, David Fizdale took over. Coach Fizdale was a fiery character who genuinely seemed to care about developing the young men he coached, on and off the court. Unfortunately, his tenure with the Memphis Grizzlies lasted just one season.

During my studies of American history, I read about the historical significance of the city of Memphis. The murder of Dr. Martin Luther King Jr. was most significant. Many of our family friends came to watch Vince play in Memphis, and part of the lure was the opportunity to visit the National Civil Rights Museum and the Lorraine Motel which is the site of the murder of Dr. King. Also in town were the Rock and Soul Museum, the Stax Museum and the home of Elvis Presley, Graceland. Taking in the sights on Beale Street was always great fun, and the food in Memphis is of the waistline-busting variety.

While in Memphis, Vince got involved in the community, speaking to students at various schools, and he made many visits to St. Jude Children's Research Hospital. Collectively, Vince and I made so many visits to the National Civil Rights Museum that we would often joke that we were really close to being able to conduct the tours. Yet, with each visit, we admitted that we saw or heard a bit of history that we had not learned during the previous visits.

While Vince was with the Memphis Grizzles, his role as a mentor became more prominent in his day-to-day activities. The Memphis squads (2014–17) consisted of several young players under the age of 25. Often Vince would be asked to mentor these young men as they were in their NBA infancy. One player was Deyonta "D.D." Davis, a 6'10", 245 lbs. center who had left Michigan State after his freshman year (2015–16). In 2016, D.D. was a rookie with the team. Often rookies who are new to an NBA team live in hotels until other accommodation is found and/or afforded. These places are usually in the city's downtown area or in close proximity to the team's practice facility or arena. There is always close contact and monitoring by team staff as they assist the player in finding a more residential neighborhood in which to stay. Sometimes, players do not have vehicles, either. Deyonta did not have one, nor did he possess a driver's license. When players are on the lower portion of the rookie payment schedule, it can take a little time for all of the pieces of the puzzle to be put in place. Vince often spoke highly of Deyonta and would comment on how this young man was very eager to learn, and he listened. Vince wanted to help D.D. get adjusted and to begin to feel comfortable in his new job, as an NBA center.

At Memphis, as in all the cities where Vince played, I would stay at his home when visiting. On one visit, I noticed that an upstairs guest bedroom was nearing the end of a renovation. The rich masculine furnishings were very nice. The room was complete with an entertainment section that included a big-screen television, music system and gaming console. As I marveled at the work that was being completed, I learned that this was all for Deyonta. Vince had created this space so that DD would have a place that felt like home. Vince would take DD to his home after practices and on off days to chill and would be there for the younger player in case he had questions about anything that was on his mind.

The 2016–17 season would be Vince's last in Memphis. Vince took the opportunity to play one season (2017–18) with the Sacramento Kings. Though Vince is not known to be a west-coast guy, he accepted the Kings' offer and thought that it would be interesting to play with his youngest team to date. Vince now got to work again with Coach Joerger, who knew that Vince would be a positive influence in the locker room and would demonstrate professionalism with this young team.

At this point in Vince's career he occasionally thought about retirement. He was 41 years old but was in great physical shape and still had the passion to play basketball at the highest level. The role of NBA basketball player was Vince's first and only full-time job. He had never been employed by any other company. He began to say publicly that there was a probability that he would play one more season.

I believe that an opportunity to return to the east coast played into the retirement thought. Part of him wanted to return closer to home. In 2018, the opportunity for Vince to play with an Eastern Conference team opened with the Atlanta Hawks organization. As always, once he signed a contract with the team, Vince got involved in many community endeavors in Atlanta, which is also another city that has connections with the civil rights movement. This civic engagement was fostered by Coach Lloyd Pierce (Coach LP). Like Coach Fizdale, Coach Pierce wanted the players to become part of the fiber of Atlanta and not just be NBA players who played the game in the city but knew nothing else about it. Coach Pierce reminisced about the Atlanta Hawks bringing Vince on to the team:

> I was hired as head coach of the Atlanta Hawks in May of 2018 and somehow became immediately involved in the recruitment of Vince to ATL once it was known that he would be looking for a new place to extend his career. Vince was known for having great locker room presence and was not in the "Ring Chasing" circuit. This bode well for me as we were building through the draft over the next two seasons. Having a veteran player with locker room presence would be very beneficial to myself as well as the organization.
>
> Class, integrity, work ethic and credibility were all undeniable from start to finish. What Vince provided exceeded our expectations. As an example, his involvement with John Collins

and helping him to expand his game behind the 3-point line was tremendous. John was a guy who rarely shot the ball in his rookie season. Our staff encouraged and allowed him to expand his shooting in volume. Vince was very instrumental in giving John all of the necessary tips to expand his game, working with him after practice, teaching him the nuances and helping him to understand the mental aspect of being "shot ready" from the 4 (power forward) position.

From a locker room presence, I personally enjoyed Vince because we just grew together, culturally. One day while we were home in Atlanta, instead of practicing, I ended up taking our young team on a field trip. I wanted to give our guys a greater understanding of what it means to live in the city of Atlanta—understanding the ties to Civil Rights, understand the important cultural contributions that were birthed in the city and just knowing where they are. We were able to visit the King Center as well as the birth home of Dr. Martin Luther King, Jr. We also visited a very famous OutKast mural for the famed group and had Atlanta artist Killer Mike and Khujo from Goddie Mob come by and speak some words about the city. Another stop was to the Slutty Vegan, an Atlanta staple owned and operated by Pinky, an up-and-coming entrepreneur.

The reason for this trip stemmed from our young guys not knowing Outkast, who is one of the most famous of all Atlanta artists, and not understanding the impact they had on the music world. Vince and I often had to fight the young guys about the classic "Old School" versus "New School" thoughts. I thought it would be fun to not only educate them but to let them hear the music. Vince and I would play Outkast during practices and workouts, while helping them to understand and appreciate the greatness of Atlanta. So, we had fun with it!

Vince had fun playing with his Hawks teammates. I could see in his smile and his body language that he was happy to be there. He seemed to be rejuvenated. I believe that a part of that came from his enjoyment of being coached by Lloyd Pierce. They were very close in age, which Vince admitted seemed a bit weird at first. But the two soon connected. Vince understood what Coach Pierce was trying to achieve with the team and wanted to be part of the mentoring process. Coach Pierce shared his thoughts with me on coaching Vince Carter:

The Making of Vince Carter

My first year as head coach, I believed that we were amongst one of the biggest differentials in age in the starting line-up, having started Trae Young and Vince... This was one of the biggest age differentials in NBA history for an opening starting line-up; although not the record. I was just fortunate to have Vince around because of the experiences needed for me being a first-year head coach with a bunch of young players.

Vince and I were both in college at the same time. We often talked about and referenced our *almost*: playing each other in college, as the Tar Heels were in Hawaii for the Maui Classic, as were my Santa Clara Broncos. I was a sophomore then in the 95–96 season. I believe North Carolina lost to Villanova in the championship game as their lone loss and we lost to Villanova to take third as our lone loss. So, had Villanova not been in the way, it would have been an even greater story to share, having previously played against Vince in college; then being able to coach him.

In this season, on November 21st, 2018, Vince achieved a major milestone. He surpassed the 25,000 career points mark with a trademark dunk. As the ball came through the nets after the dunk and bounced from the floor, Vince caught it with both hands, held his head back, closed his eyes and exhaled. The game was halted for a few moments as the players from both teams, and fans, congratulated Vince on this enormous feat. Ironically, this achievement came in a game where the Hawks hosted the Toronto Raptors.

After the 2018–19 season, Vince wanted one more opportunity to play with the Atlanta Hawks. He got it. There was only one more season to play, to break the all-time record for years played in the National Basketball Association. If Vince played in an NBA game in January of 2020, the record was his. On January 6th, 2020, the Hawks hosted the Denver Nuggets and Vince played over 18 minutes in the game, breaking the NBA longevity record. The Hawks lost, but Vince had passed a milestone.

Vince was looking to play out the season in Atlanta, when fate threw the league, and the world, a curve ball. On March 11th 2020, the Atlanta Hawks hosted the New York Knicks.

The world was reeling from an outbreak of the coronavirus coined COVID-19. This highly infectious disease had infiltrated the National Basketball Association. That morning, the top infectious disease expert Dr. Anthony Fauci testified before Congress that the coronavirus outbreak in the United States would get much worse. By noon, the World Health Organization officially declared COVID-19 a pandemic. But it wasn't obvious what this meant for the NBA yet. The NBA league office was still in wait-and-see mode.

By approximately 2:00 p.m. the Golden State Warriors made the decision to play their scheduled March 12th game against the Brooklyn Nets, but without fans in attendance. By the end of the same day, all NCAA basketball tournaments were cancelled, which was a huge deal. At 7:00 p.m., the Atlanta Hawks began their home game against the New York Knicks. By half-time, bad news began to circulate throughout State Farm Arena. It was just prior to 8:30 p.m. when fans, including me, began receiving mobile device notifications that the Oklahoma City Thunder vs. Utah Jazz game was canceled due to a positive COVID-19 test for Utah Jazz center Rudy Gobert. Meanwhile in Atlanta, as fans and some of the Hawks staff were following the developments of the pandemic on their mobile devices, it became apparent to the Hawks players and coaching staff that this could, indeed, be Vince Carter's last game. At approximately 10:30 p.m., Vince's career came to a sudden end. With 12.6 seconds left in the game, Vince got his final bucket—a 3-pointer from the top of the key. The assist went to Trey Young. The game ended in overtime with the Hawks losing 136–131.

The NBA announced that after the last scheduled game on March 11th, 2020, the remainder of the season would be suspended. Since Vince had already announced that this season would be his last, he said that this felt like some sort of sign that it was the end. He felt the suspension of play due to COVID actually lessened the blow of the reality of retirement. Vince had been looking forward to playing his final games in front of appreciative crowds at many arenas across the country as part of his farewell tour—the same kind of final tour that Kobe Bryant and Dwayne Wade experienced in their final seasons. At many of those away games, Kobe and D-Wade received standing ovations from the crowd. Vince was not sure what to expect, but he sure didn't expect COVID.

In the midst of the COVID-19 unknown, Coach Pierce had these thoughts:

> One of the toughest parts about the ending of Vince's career was the inability to be a part of the *closure. All great players* deserve a final goodbye to the game. Vince had the unusual ending due to the pandemic. This kept him from receiving his *final goodbye* from various NBA cities, many teams and numerous fans that would have loved to see him one last time. From the start of the season, it just wasn't in the cards for him to receive the proper send-off. Due to the birth of his daughter, Vince was unable to head west with us early in the season to receive the proper send-offs that the Los Angeles teams fans would have given him. He missed what would have been a great send-off in the city of Phoenix where he had a tremendous impact with the Suns.

As I think back on it, this low-key departure was in harmony with who Vince truly is. He didn't play the game for the accolades or the celebrations. He always played with passion, flare, class, and respect. Although the deserved ending was denied, only a person like Vince could truly handle that and not seek it. It was particularly disappointing, though, that the pandemic-shortened season denied us a final trip back to Toronto, which had been scheduled in April 2020 just a week shy of season's end. That would have been a very emotional, touching tribute from the beloved Toronto and Canadian fans, whose hearts Vince won early, bringing basketball a new star before they had ever even had one! I truly feel like the NBA and the basketball world was denied a special night. I am thankful that Vince was able to get his 25,000th point versus the Raptors on a dunk at the end of the game in 2018. It seemed fitting to have a monumental moment against his former team.

Indeed, this was the end of Vince's 22-year NBA career. In my opinion, Vince's high school basketball coach, Charles Brinkerhoff, summed up his career the best:

> Vince developed in his career to accentuate the talent he has and knowledge he gained to play a variety of roles in the NBA from Superstar to Mentor. Vince "officially" retired on June 25th, 2020. Of course, the continuation of that catharsis has set him on a course to be as good a television game analyst as he was a player. As a basketball player, Vince's accolades are well documented. At a different level, though, I would like to more often hear the term "artist" used to describe his impact and playing style. His favorite players, such as Julius Erving, were graceful and played with a certain flair. In my opinion, Vince continued and expanded that tradition by playing at all levels with grace, fluidity, and style that made for unforgettable fan memories. I am very proud of Vince for many things. One of the things I am proud of Vince for, late in his career, was when he assumed the role of mentor to younger players. There are so many players in the NBA currently that have Vince to thank for teaching them how to be professional athletes… on the court and off."

I couldn't agree more. What a ride!

The Making of Vince Carter

13

Vices Everywhere (and You Love Some of Them)

Vince's participation in high school sports started the process that propelled him into the national spotlight. This happened before the internet became popular, so in the beginning he was mostly known to fans who truly cared about high school and college basketball. Vince had a lot of local fans back then, but none that I'd ever describe as "groupies". Sure, there were some high school girls who wanted to date Vince and pursued him in unsubtle ways. But generally Vince understood that their motives were more about being popular and being seen with the perfect jock boyfriend than possessing a genuine, lasting interest in him.

Once Vince began playing basketball at that national powerhouse the University of North Carolina at Chapel Hill, he was becoming a household name to fans across the country. The team's home games typically had a whopping 20,000 plus fans in attendance. That's right, the Dean Smith Center, which everyone called the "Dean Dome," had a capacity to host up to 21,175 fans, and usually the home games sold out. I remember that after one game at the Dean Dome I noticed how Vince's burgeoning stardom began to attract a different kind of fan from anything I had known before. When I was in town watching my son play, my usual habit after the game was to wait for him in the basketball office in the Dean Dome. From there, I could see Vince emerge from the locker room. There were always family members of other players, and some fans around me, also waiting for the players to leave the locker room. Most of the fans were fellow UNC college students, or Chapel Hill locals, including kids who just wanted a glimpse of the Tar Heels' star players. The more ambitious among the fans wanted autographs from the players. This was right before cell phones with decent cameras became common, so selfies were still a rarity back then. A third type of fan also sometimes awaited Vince: this was the type I had never encountered before. They wanted something a little extra.

One day, while waiting after the game for Vince, I noticed a group of attractive young ladies who really stood out. This was because they didn't look like college students or townies at all, but like they were models going to the club on a Saturday night in a big city somewhere, with their tiny dresses, full-on hair and makeup, and high heels. They were done up like they were in Miami's South Beach waiting for NBA players to hit the club—except they were in a preppy college town targeting young men who were, at minimum, eight to ten years their junior. Young men, many still teenagers, who probably had homework due in class the next day. I'm guessing the ladies wanted to catch a star athlete boyfriend on the way up—and, to be fair, Chapel Hill was a good place for their hunt. I tried to reserve judgement.

Then I actually heard one of the well-coiffed young ladies announce that she was there for Vince Carter, as if she knew him well, and wanted to know him even better. She clearly had no idea who I was, or she wouldn't have been that bold. Well, I don't *think* she would—but, after all, you have to be pretty bold to target young men like that. Vince was only 19 years old when this event occurred.

    Needless to say, I was a bit stunned. I wasn't sure if I should approach the group of ladies and announce myself, or tell them off, or what. Should I go, "Excuse me, I'm Vince's mom, is he a close friend of yours?" or something like that, to let them know that I was on to them? They had name-checked my son, so confronting them was fair game. I decided it was best, no matter what, not to make a scene. I didn't want to cause any embarrassment for anyone, including myself, Vince, or his teammates such as Antawn and Ademola whom I regarded as my family, too. Being the protective mom that I am, though, I still needed to do something. As Vince was approaching the basketball office, I alerted him that the women were waiting for him. He took a quick peek through the glass door and remarked, "I don't know them."

    It was customary for the Tar Heels basketball players to be escorted, by security, to their vehicles in the nearby parking lot. These guys are bombarded by adoring fans before and after every game. Sometimes these strangers are over the top in their show of admiration. Vince was usually the last player out of the locker room. Security was accustomed to this. I could tell that they had seen the women lurking, too. Vince and I, along with the two-man security escorts, got to his vehicle and off we went.

    When I asked Vince whether he knew the group, he looked weirded out and confused. I may or may not have given the ladies a smug little smile on the way to the car as I watched their smiles deflate. If I did, can you blame me? I guess that was the day I learned what "jersey chasing" was, and that it was a popular sport among certain pretty young women who frequent college towns.

    If what I saw that day mildly surprised me, then I was in for more shock when Vince joined the NBA. Of course, winning the NBA's Slam Dunk Contest in 2000 and being named the Rookie-of-the-Year elevated his fame off the charts. With the many accolades came other stuff—the stuff that happens when some entitled people decide that an athlete can be their pathway to something better.

Once Vince entered the NBA, we began to hear that we had more "cousins" than one could shake a stick at. Most members of our legitimate small family had an encounter with someone who claimed to know a person that said he or she was a "cousin" of the Carter family. The Vince Carter million-dollar smile did not help matters either. Women were coming from every corner, and they were not after that smile. That group of finely dressed young ladies outside the Dean Dome was a warmup for the reality of the NBA.

As the person whose responsibility was to oversee the off-court facets of Vince's career, I was part of the NBA world for a few decades. I heard some intriguing stories about players and their women: like the players that had two families—the official married one, and the other one in a different city where the team played on the road. I even know of one player who had more than two families. None of these arrangements ever get discussed in the media, and that's probably for the best. I sometimes marvel at how relatively non-complicated Vince's personal life was during his active NBA years.

Later I learned of female groups that coached each other on "how to nab a professional athlete." There were stories of women who claimed they were with child, and the player, at times, seemed baffled. There is a reason paternity tests exist. Use them!

The salaries of professional athletes are public. At times, family members seek to make plans predicated on the earnings of these athletes. The expectations of family and friends can at times show a negative side of the ones you love.

Pro athletes must understand that it is imperative not to

spend money that they don't have. There are so many variables affecting the earnings of athletes. Depending on the nature of the athlete's contract, the salary may not be guaranteed. Injuries can also strike at any time. As with death and taxes, there is a certainty that, sooner or later, the end of an athlete's professional playing career will come. If there is one thing I have learned it's that pro athletes rarely retire from their sport on their own terms. At any given time, there are former All-Star NBA players who are still in the League but clearly struggle with the reality that they are in the fading years of their career and are not as good as they once were. Their roles have diminished, but their egos have not.

Having a solid financial plan is a must for any pro athlete. Money must be invested wisely, because the future for any professional athlete is by default uncertain. Vince did not have a problem with this. The problem was that sometimes it's hard figuring out what comprises a wise business plan or opportunity. Athletes are bombarded by colleagues and so-called "friends" who want them to invest in one scheme or another.

From the start, Vince would send all investment requests to me. My degrees in business helped me to navigate and say no with a straight face to the sketchier requests. I was lucky that Vince did not feel that he owed anyone other than his parents and God for the position in which he found himself. From my perspective, he did not owe his parents anything. We did what parents are supposed to do. He never felt beholden to invest in a venture just because it was presented by family or anyone he knew from inside or outside the NBA world.

If you have money, it won't take long before propositions for "business deals that you can't refuse" will come along. My response to these is "I have never seen a deal that I could not refuse." Again, Vince would send all deals to me and his agent. Those proposals that were absurd were vetoed by me and never reached the rest of Team Carter.

Vices can also come in disguises. Fans are very much appreciated by most athletes. The roar of the crowd usually provides the juice that players need to perform at their highest level. There are times, however, when fans just don't think about what the players are really going through. They ignore the fact that the players are human and need privacy, just as they do. I still wear the "bad girl" hat when Vince and his family are out dining and, between bites, we are interrupted with autograph or photo requests. I can recall one time when my family and I were attending a funeral. Being passed down the church's pew was the funeral program with an autograph request along with it. All I could think of was *what the hell is going on?* I intercepted the program and U-turned it back down the pew.

After a few years of my escalated salary as the chief executive officer of Vince's company, Visions in Flight, Inc., I discovered, or rather, began to indulge in, a certain vice, namely a taste for fashion and nice vehicles. I've always had a taste for fine clothes, handbags, shoes and jewelry. Still do. But I also always knew my financial place. When I was a public-school teacher with a teacher husband, I simply did not have the means for high-end designer clothes and handbags. I simply didn't buy those things. I pursued fashion wisely. I tried always to buy well-made clothes that were well priced and would be stylish for ever. Every year my husband might treat me to a luxury gift, like nice perfume for my birthday, or I might save up for a Caribbean cruise, but these were special, infrequent occasions. Once we had to start paying for Vince's basketball camps and AAU fees during his high school days, I put the cruises on hold as already mentioned.

While working as a teacher, I strove to always look as put together as possible—I thought this was important, as I was a business instructor. I wanted to set an example of what real-world business people looked like. I wore what

I would call "dress casual" outfits. I never wore khakis or sweatshirts to school, even on the casual Fridays where some teachers dressed way down. Even if I looked dressy for school, however, I also stayed strictly within my means and limited clothes budget. The only luxury purchase I ever made in my teaching days was a nice car. I carefully budgeted to be able to afford a nicer vehicle. It was never an impulse buy, and I made sure I always found a great deal.

When Vince started playing in college, my fashion choices and expenses were still modest. Chapel Hill had some great boutiques where they sold Tar Heels themed knit sweaters that were much fancier than most college branded garb. My typical Dean Dome wardrobe was one of these boutique sweaters and a nice pair of slacks. My clothes were dressier than those of some of the parents, but still within the normal range.

Once I started my new chief executive officer career, I began to get comfortable with my heightened salary, which was roughly four to eight times what it had previously been, depending on the year and the nature of my responsibilities. Generally, Vince's agents handled the brunt of his NBA deal making, while I focused more on his investment strategy, sponsorships and endorsement deals. Vince's agents always kept me in the loop on the NBA contract negotiating side of things.

While in Toronto, I remember going to the Eaton Centre, walking among its many high-end boutique stores, and realizing that I could finally afford the luxury goods that were offered. At first, I was hesitant to buy, because although I knew I had more money in the moment, I didn't know how long this income was sustainable. Again, I knew NBA careers could be very short for a variety of reasons. For a while, I still mostly window shopped. I didn't want a habit I couldn't sustain.

It wasn't long before I had become a minor fixture at the Raptors' home games at the Air Canada Centre in Toronto.

The Making of Vince Carter

In the arena, the camera operators sometimes cut to a close-up of me in the stands rooting for my son and the team. This would appear on the "jumbotron," the huge four-sided TV display that hangs in the center of the arena for all the fans to see. The Raptors' media team would announce that I was Vince's mom. Whenever they did this, it often made the live game feed as well, so fans in attendance and at home watching the game on TV began to know who I was. I was a bit ambivalent about this; I appreciated the attention, but I also became a bit self-conscious about it. They started doing this for every home game I attended, whether I liked it or not.

Then, during one home game in early 1999, the camera cut to me when I was wearing a truly regrettable outfit. I think it was a Raptors' sweatshirt and jeans. It just wasn't a good look. I recall being truly embarrassed seeing myself looking this way on the jumbotron. I resolved to never look this way on camera again.

The next time I visited the Eaton Centre or any of the other amazing boutiques, I was there to buy. The Centre had every designer shop you could imagine, and I was on a mission to look good. Vince was becoming the team's franchise player, so I was determined to be a great franchise mom. I remember going to the boutiques and finding outfits that not only flattered my figure but that I thought would look great in any circumstance. I started dressing up for the games. My hair and makeup were always on point. I wore designer clothes, handbags, and shoes. I was new to the world of expensive jewelry and was blown away by the luxurious offerings at stores like Royal de Versailles. I don't recall what my early jewelry purchases were, but I do remember they were a world apart from anything I could afford on a teacher's salary. I sometimes got looks from fans in sweatshirts who sat near me; they were like, "Why is she so dressed up for a game?" But these fans did not know what it was like to look terrible on the jumbotron and live game feed. Soon, looking great for the games became my thing, and I think fans appreciated it.

  When I started buying nicer things, I still felt like I was on a limited budget, because Vince was still new to the League. As Vince's career progressed, and the multi-million-dollar contracts became normal, I felt a little more emboldened. I developed a sometimes regrettable habit of not looking at prices before I bought items. I would see something I liked in a designer boutique, grab it, and immediately take it to the cashier. I admit I sometimes suffered serious sticker shock doing this, no matter how much I was earning. I do not recommend this habit, as it was something I eventually had to unlearn as Vince's pro career wound down. That was a vice, not a virtue.

  Fashion was my vice, but I only pursued it with my own money. Period. I was extremely careful with Vince's money and investments. I and the financial team steered him in a way that set him up quite well financially for life. In my managing career, I made one relatively minor financial misstep and invested a sizeable, though comparatively modest, sum in a bogus venture. I think I did this because the person who came to me with the investment request was none other than Vince's first agent, a man whom we had come to trust with Vince's NBA deals. The agent wanted millions from Vince for the venture, which was a kind of Ponzi scheme, but I was cautious and only invested 200K. Nevertheless, it was still an error of judgement and one that I will never forget. It never happened again. The agent, meanwhile, eventually ended up serving time in prison for these criminal schemes. There were several other athletes as well, who lost a lot more money. Why an agent who was so successful resorted to fraud remains a mystery to me.

  The bottom line is that there must be someone who is knowledgeable *and* has the best interests of the athlete at heart in the primary position of managing the career. The athlete does not need to be saddled with the research necessary to make sound decisions about investments, but the manager must be vigilant constantly. That being said, there should never be any blanket decisions or agreements made in isolation from the athlete. After all, it is his or her reputation and future financial security that are on the line. I think I found a balance with Vince that worked well for us both and kept errors in check.

14

Here's What I Know

So here we are. Thus far in this journey, I have learned numerous things that helped me raise a family, build multiple careers, and build a life I am very proud of. I hope that my sharing of my path will, at least, cause you to pause and think about a possible alternate route through your journey in life. One thing I haven't dwelled on much is my spiritual development in life. But it's an important factor in my success, and in the success of my son.

Prayer has been my guiding principle throughout my life; especially once my son Vince went to college. When Vince left home, our family life became more complicated, in that he began his public journey to the NBA, and all that entailed. My life, conversely, simplified somewhat, in that I suddenly had fewer direct parenting responsibilities, like shuttling kids to practice, college visits, and dealing with the non-stop demands of the recruitment process. There were many times when I called upon God for answers in my early life, but as I grew older I prayed even more. Sometimes I prayed to the point that I heard God tell me that He had to listen to others and promised to get back to me. Yes, I sometimes felt like God put me and my worries on hold. I know there were times I wore God out with my petitions. But God always had my back, and in one way or another showed me the best path. This is the only way I believed my family and I survived sometimes.

People often remark about Vince that he had no blemishes on his career in high school, college, or the NBA; that he was always a standup guy who behaved responsibly and professionally. I have sometimes been given credit for Vince's righteousness, but I don't deserve this. Again, I tell you that it is by the grace of God that this is so. When I didn't know which way to turn and didn't have the answer, I prayed, and prayed some more, and then took a hot shower. Every time I prayed and quietly reflected on my troubles and issues, eventually the best path became clear. There are many different spiritual pathways. I recommend finding one that keeps you honest, humble, respectful, and loving in all things.

As a parent, we want the best for our children. Have you ever stopped to ask yourself what *is* "the best"? I've learned that playing the "what if" game and backing it up with research is extremely prudent. By "what if" I mean charting out all possible outcomes and futures that might come with any major decision. It forces one to look at different sides of the concern. If you have more than one child, don't throw them all in the same basket. My sons are two years, ten months apart in age. Though they were raised in the same household, by the same rules, there are many areas where they are as different as night and day. As a parent, you have to respect those differences and develop methods of raising each child in a way that respects each on his or her own terms. As I look back, I could have done a better job at this one. I wasn't as good as I should have been at recognizing how different my boys were, and how what worked for one sometimes needed to be modified for the other.

Raising two male athletes who, due to their ages, were

Here's What I Know

always in different leagues, had its challenges. Moms and dads get tired. My husband and I worked full-time as educators, but we were determined to be there for the boys. It is imperative that you find that energy from somewhere. You just *must* find it! You will not be able to get those years back. Once they are gone, they are gone. Usually, we want our children to have a better life than we had. But what does this mean? As I look back, I realize that I didn't have a tough life as a youngster. I had everything that I needed and most of the things that I wanted. But society makes us believe that we are not great parents if we don't adopt this cliché of giving our children everything. Listen to me: as I have lived and learned, I realize that in most cases this has weakened our children.

My parents did not allow my sisters or me to work while in high school. They did not want us girls to be able to use work as an excuse for unacceptable grades. We had one job while growing up—to get good grades and go to college. So, fast forward. I did not permit my sons to work while in high school or college. With their hectic multi-sport schedules, they did not have time to work and go to school as well. Something had to give, right? Working was not going to be an excuse for not measuring up to the minimum 3.0 grade point average of the Carter household. Doing well in school was always the most important thing.

Even if your child is an elite athlete, I strongly recommend making sure they understand how doing well in school can facilitate their dreams just as much as sports can, with much less risk. Vince, with his God-given athletic talent and hard work, was able to beat the odds and have a successful long-lived pro sports career. But he represents the exception to the rule. Sport careers are not guaranteed, and certainly not a 22-year professional one.

At any given time, there are roughly 450 players in the NBA proper, not including two-way contract players who are paid less and can be cut at any time. As I write this, since the NBA was founded in the late 1940s more than seven decades ago, there have been roughly 5000 players in total who have played in an NBA game. That's it: 5000. Considering millions of boys and girls play high school and AAU basketball each year, the odds are wildly stacked against them having a pro career. As a result, I never based my success as a parent on whether or not my sons went pro. That would have been foolish. I judged my success on whether or not they graduated from college. That was my real marker of achievement.

There are times when your young athlete will need to lean heavily on you. The words that you say, or the actions you take, could make or break his or her chance at playing in college or making a career in sports. But you'll never fully understand your impact. You have so much power as a parent, but unfortunately you don't get a map. You just don't know the impact of your words and actions. Be careful and wise in how you communicate. Always have a positive goal in mind, especially when engaging in tough love.

I will always be an educator at heart. During the past 20 years I have noticed that young people want to be seen and heard. They have a robust way of going about their missions. They are vocal. They are active. Personally I am thankful that these young people are not sitting still. They are being proactive in making positive changes.

In general, we do a disservice to people, including our children, when we constantly tell them what they want to hear when we know it is not the truth. Sometimes the truth can be hard to swallow. But the truth is the truth! Once the truth is told, the next moves are to make the truth better. My philosophy is that there is nothing that I can't, at least, make better (if not solve in its entirety).

Recently Antawn Jamison, Vince's UNC teammate, told me that I was unlike most sports parents in that I hadn't just presented uncritical praise to my son and the other guys on the team. He appreciated that I had always been honest.

I had told the players when they needed to work harder or focus more. After a team loss, for example, other parents would tell the boys some form of, "you still played great," or "you can't win them all," or "you'll win the next time!" Meanwhile, I would offer my son, and the other players I knew well, constructive criticism, and make suggestions for improvement. I believe this was far more helpful than only telling them what they wanted to hear.

As your athlete moves to the next level in the sport, the competition is more challenging. That's a given in sports. Your athlete's stats may not roll in like they once did, and it's best to figure out everything your athlete can do to improve. Doing the little things in sports can make the difference in wins and losses. In basketball, chasing loose balls, setting screens, and rebounding are just as important as scoring the basket. After all, you can't score until you have the ball. The efforts made that don't make it to the stat sheet are often called "the intangibles."

The intangibles also matter off the court or field. Does your athlete do well in school? Are they respectful of their elders? Do they always take responsibility for their actions? Do they fully recognize and appreciate opportunities? These intangibles can be both learned and improved upon. But it's up to the athlete. Even if an athlete "makes it," the learning curve never ends. I watched my son transition from a franchise player ("the guy") to, in the last part of his career, being a role player coming off the bench. Making this humbling transition provided Vince with extra years, and millions more dollars earned, in the League. He holds the record for the longest NBA career ever in part because he consistently adapted to new team situations and realities, while never letting his ego get in the way.

The best of the best athletes know how to stretch themselves. Vince is, traditionally, a shooting guard—sometimes referred to as a big guard or two-guard. In this day of positionless basketball, wherever the needs were, coaches felt comfortable in putting him in those positions. Surprisingly to me, in the latter years of his career, Vince often played at the power-forward position. Undersized, yes, but he held his own. That's stretching for the good of the team. For Vince to find success in this situation, he had to be a student of the game. He had to expand beyond his natural scoring abilities and optimize his defense. His quickness and basketball acumen helped to offset the vast difference in size of his opponent. Vince did what he needed to help the team. He always wanted to be a basketball player that plays in every game. Vince was not at all interested in being a decoration at the end of the bench for the sake of chasing a ring.

Vince also learned the art of mentorship. He has always liked helping others, especially kids, but doing so in a pro team environment is a much more complex undertaking. In order to be a great mentor in the NBA, you have to manage egos, favoritism, team politics, and a whole host of other factors beyond athletics. Vince managed to navigate this tricky environment by putting his own ego on a shelf and being open and relatable to younger players.

Veterans who teach younger players the ropes represent another "intangible." Older players who mentor are critical to a team's success, and good general managers and coaches recognize this. I encourage sports parents to become mentors to their children. Pass along your wisdom and best life lessons to your kids.

At times, life can be a rat race. When you are an involved parent, the "to do" list seems to never end. When you are the parent of student-athletes, that list is so much more daunting. But if you put your mind to it, you can do it. I remember how overwhelmed I felt when I was driving Vince to games and practice, while he did his homework in the car. We made it work, even though it sometimes felt like we were in the middle of a storm. Because we lived in Central Florida, sometimes we were literally in the middle of an actual storm, too. But again, we made it work.

When you know better, you do better. In the midst of these important storms, you must take the time to enjoy the view. Don't get so busy making a living that you forget to make a life, and not only for your child, but also for yourself and your family. The day will come when there will be that first time that you stop and wonder where it all has gone. Your child will grow into an adult and there will be nothing left of their early days except memories—and of course the fruits of their efforts, and of yours. I hope that the overwhelming majority of the memories are beautiful and that you will have no cause for regret. It's important to live life to the fullest while you can because you never know what will happen next.

Even if your child never makes the pros, the ride is worth it. Establishing good habits and a strong work ethic in your child will pay off for the rest of their lives. Even after his retirement, my son has many new opportunities and potential career paths because he is well rounded and learned skills that matter off court. He also developed all-important people skills and made many lifelong friends in the League and beyond.

Vince first became friends with the great NBA Hall-of-Famer Kobe Bryant when they were teenagers playing AAU basketball together. Their friendship only grew over the years. Kobe went to the NBA right out of high school, while Vince became a student-athlete at the University of North Carolina. Even though Vince was slightly older than Kobe, he often felt like Kobe was his mentor because of his non-stop drive and determination to win. Vince was inspired by Kobe's legendary willpower.

After Vince declared that the 2019–20 season would be his last, Kobe and Vince had promised to get together to talk about retirement, like old friends, like old times. According to Vince, Kobe told him to enjoy retirement and pursue his other interests. He was adamant that a rich life awaited Vince after the NBA. Of course, Vince had several more questions at this point, so they promised to talk again soon. But fate intervened in a tragic way.

Kobe died in a helicopter crash in Los Angeles County, on January 26th, 2020. He was only 41 years old. The date of the tragedy was Vince's 43rd birthday, so the news of Kobe's death was extra devastating to him. For Vince and our family there was no celebrating of that birthday. Vince told me, "Now on my birthday I will always think of what happened to Kobe first. This is tough." Kobe's passing was another reminder of how short and unpredictable life is. How we must savor it while we live it.

Not long after Kobe died, fate intervened again in an unexpected way. Vince's last NBA game was March 11th, 2020, when the League's season ended prematurely because of COVID. The season stopping in March was a shock to everyone, but especially to Vince, who'd declared the season his last. That was also tough, but I think Kobe's positive words about retirement helped Vince accept the sudden situation without doubts or regrets.

You might think that my proudest moment as a parent would have something to do with basketball. Like Vince's great seasons in high school and UNC, or when his NBA teams went deep into the playoffs, or when he won Olympic Gold. You'd be wrong. I loved all those times, but when Vince graduated from college, I felt pride swell in me that was unlike anything else I have ever felt.

As you know, Vince and I had an agreement that, whatever NBA offers he received, or however his pro career played out, he would someday go back to school and get his bachelor's degree. This was the napkin agreement that we made on his way to college as an 18-year-old. I have also related how, after Vince was drafted into the NBA, he diligently attended summer school, in person, for three terms at the University of North Carolina. Keep in mind that these studies happened *after* he was a multi-millionaire. Once all academic requirements were completed, Vince was eligible to graduate from UNC. He only needed to order his cap and his gown, and pay for his campus parking tickets (I was stunned by the cost of the latter!) Vince wanted to graduate like a regular student, in cap and gown, and walk in the traditional ceremony.

Our family was extremely proud of the commitment Vince made. Certainly, a man in his position could spend his summers engaged in more glamorous activities and take lavish vacations. Instead, Vince put receiving his college degree at the top of his "to do" list and kept his promise to me. May 20th, 2001, was one of the most precious days of my life. My son received his bachelor's degree, and I was there to see him enter Kenan Stadium adorned in his Carolina Blue cap and gown amongst all the other graduates and academicians.

As I close my eyes and take a very deep breath, I see those moments that will always mean the most to me. The days that my sons, Vincent and Christopher, were born. The moment I realized that Vincent and his high school basketball team had made it back to the Florida State Championship game and won! The moment I heard, "With the fifth pick of the NBA draft, the Golden State Warriors select Vince Carter." The first time I saw Vince in his USA Olympic uniform; and later that gold medal being put around his neck as he stood on the podium. The pounding in my chest and the tears in my eyes when my son, Vincent Lamar Carter, entered the stadium in his Carolina Blue cap and gown to receive his bachelor's degree. As my eyes are closed, I can see Vince hoisting the trophy and being declared the winner of the 2000 NBA Slam Dunk Contest. The moments my grandchildren, Kai Michelle, Vincent Lamar and Vayle Elizabeth were born; I can see each one. I can see Vince's last shot as an NBA player on March 11th, 2020.

And now, I wait. I wait for the day that Vince receives the announcement that he has been selected to the Naismith Basketball Hall of Fame. Then, we will have come full circle.

From a youngster, Vince has dreamed of playing at the highest level, in the National Basketball Association. According to Vince, he has never dreamed of being inducted into the Hall of Fame. Who would have the audacity to do that? But I feel, with God, all things are possible. This is my prayer.

15
What's Next

It's amazing to me that even though Vincent Lamar Carter holds the record for the longest active NBA playing career he is still a relatively young man. Vince retired at age 43, which is ancient in NBA player years, but it's young for most careers. It's a stark reminder that every athlete's playing career is finite. No matter how good you are, or how well you adapt, a pro athlete career is not going to last into old age. My son was blessed to be able to play 1541 NBA games in total, the third most in the history of the League. I watched almost all of my son's games, either in person or on TV, and it was quite the journey for me, too.

Vince is enjoying his NBA retirement. Nowadays, his favorite activities revolve around finally being able to be a more normal dad. After two decades of being on the move for work, and switching cities on the regular, my elder son loves nothing more than dropping his kids off at school, then picking them up later. Or taking his kids to practice and lessons or helping them with homework. He loves doing the basic parent stuff. The very things I once juggled, that sometimes overwhelmed me and drove me to distraction, he flat-out loves to do. Good for him.

In September 2020, Vince signed a multi-year deal with the US sports channel ESPN (Disney is the parent company), serving as a basketball analyst. He takes this job as seriously as he did being a professional basketball player. He works as a "color analyst" now, or the announcer who provides background info and stats on players during game broadcasts. Although Vince is provided with some information and talking points by producers, he nevertheless conducts his own research before each game.

Prior to each game broadcast, Vince makes a chart showing all the players of each team, indicates their playmaking habits and key stats, and notes interesting factoids. His process reminds me of the charts I made back during his college recruitment days that included every piece of information I had about every school and coach that sought to recruit Vince. It makes me wonder whether chart-making tendencies are genetic! Ha ha!

Though he doesn't talk about it much, it is important to Vince to be enshrined one day in the Naismith Basketball Hall of Fame. As of December 2017, players, retired coaches and referees are eligible for this career-defining distinction, from at least three full seasons after fully retiring. A 24-member screening committee comprising Hall of Famers, basketball executives and administrators, members of the media and other experts in the game of basketball, annually votes on those to be inducted. A finalist must get a minimum of 18 votes from the committee to be enshrined. I am hopeful that the basketball gods, and their earthly representatives, will smile upon Vince.

Since his playing days ended, Vince has also had more time to hone his golf skills. He has often lamented that there are days when he plays well on the golf course and then there are days when the golf course plays him and teaches him new lessons in patience and humility. Overall, he's improving his golf game, and he loves nothing more than playing rounds with his former NBA and college buddies.

Vince and I are still both active in his non-profit organization, the Embassy of Hope Foundation, that he founded in 1998. In the two decades plus that it has existed, Embassy of Hope has helped many young people, mostly from Central Florida, afford to go to college. It's especially rewarding when I see recipients of our scholarships thrive in our local community. Watching people you've helped coming into their own, and giving back, is a beautiful thing.

I'm now enjoying my new role as "Mimi"—grandmother—in my semi-retirement mode. I remember thinking that my mom, who was very strict with me and my sisters, was noticeably less strict, even indulgent, with her grandkids Vince, Chris and Tiffany. Well now I'm that person with my amazing grandkids. Time doesn't just conquer all, it also mellows out most people, me included.

Professionally, as someone of normal retirement age, I'm trying to do less, but sometimes I don't know how. Maybe finishing this book will help me out. But I already have thoughts to write a children's book next—a book that I hope will entertain kids while teaching them about the importance of learning, being kind, helping others, loyalty, and just being the best that they can be every day. As already stated, I believe that once you know better, you should do better. My mom said: "Once a teacher, always a teacher." My mom was right more often than I like admitting even now. Her love of teaching and learning was the bedrock on which my sisters and I built our families. It served us well.

I hope that in the stories and anecdotes I've shared here I've passed along some of my most important life lessons to you—the lessons that helped me as a sports parent to guide Vince into being an exceptional athlete and person.

But, as I've learned, even if you do everything right it's not easy to raise an elite athlete. There will always be time, school, training, and money issues, and, as I said, you don't get a map. But those of us who've gone though it can at least impart some of our knowledge and provide inspiration. Your kids will often be so caught up in their own lives that they may not appreciate the sacrifices you make, or even notice all the things you do for them. But as a fellow sports parent, I know how important you are. I believe in you and wish you all the best in the world.

Afterword

Vince Carter played his last NBA game on March 11th, 2020. The COVID pandemic had just become a reality for NBA players. On that evening, some teams canceled games while others suddenly halted them with fans already in the arena. Vince and the Atlanta Hawks did complete the game against the New York Knicks. The COVID pandemic news began to spread throughout the arena. Coaches sitting on both benches began to receive alerts on their mobile phones. It wasn't long before players on the bench heard the whispers, and the news was confirmed at half time while players were in the locker room. It was a bizarre but memorable endpoint to a truly remarkable career.

The Making of Vince Carter

Vince Carter's Career Data and Statistics

Position: shooting guard/small forward
Height/Weight: 6'6"/220 lbs.
Born: January 26, 1977, in Daytona Beach, FL, USA at Halifax Hospital
High School: Mainland High School in Daytona Beach, FL
College: University of North Carolina (left after his junior year in 1998, took summer classes and graduated May 2021)
Nicknames: Vinsanity, Half-Man Half-Amazing, VC, Elevator Man, Florida Flash
Drafted by: Golden State Warriors at #5 in the first round of the 1998 NBA
Jersey Numbers: 15 (Raptors, Nets, Magic, Grizzlies, Kings, Hawks); 25 (Suns, Mavericks)
NBA Seasons: 22 (holds NBA record)
NBA Playoffs: 11
All-Star: 8 (played 7)

Vince has played with or against 1672 individual players in his NBA career, more than any other player in the history of the league (source: nba.com).

Regular NBA Season Stats

GP: 1541 GS: 982 3 PT: 2290–6168 3P%: 37.1 FT: 4852–6082 FT%: 79.8
OR: 1658 DR: 4948 REB: 6606 AST: 4714 BLK: 888 STL: 1530 PF: 3995
TO: 2590 PTS: 25728

Miscellaneous NBA Regular Season Stats

DD2: 90 TD3: 5 EJECT: 5 TECH: 94 FLAG: 6 AST/TO: 1.8 STL/TO: 0.6

Glossary

3P%: 3-point field goal percentage
3PT: 3-point field goals made/attempted per game
AST: assists per game
AST/TO: assist to turnover ratio
BLK: blocks per game
DD2: double-double DR: defensive rebounds per game
EJECT: ejections
FG: field goals made/attempted per game
FG%: field goal percentage
FLAG: flagrant fouls
FT: free throws made/attempted per game
FT%: free throw percentage
GP: games played
GS: games started
MIN: minutes per game
OR: offensive rebounds per game
PF: fouls per game
PTS: points per game
REB: rebounds per game
STL: steals per game

STL/TO: steals to turnover ratio
T3: triple double
TECH: technical fouls
TO: turnovers per game

Vince's Rankings

NBA All-Time Leaders: Vince Carter (as of May 2021)
Points: 19th (1541)
Free Throw Attempts: 42nd (6082)
Free Throws Made: 40th (4852)
Number of NBA Games Played: One of the most impressive of Vince's stats. In an era when players are more plagued by injuries, this stat offers a concise measurement of stamina, longevity, conditioning, and endurance. Vince has played in 1629 (1541 regular season: 88 playoff) games.
Field Goals Attempted: 12th (21,339)
Field Goals Made: 21st (9293)
3PA: 6th (6168)
3PM: 6th (2290)
Steals: 43rd (1530)
TOV: 47th (2590)
Minutes—15th (46,370)
Holds NBA Record for Most 3-Point Goals in a Half (8)

Vince's NBA Teams

Toronto Raptors (1998–2004)
New Jersey Nets (2004–09)
Orlando Magic (2009–10)
Phoenix Suns (2010–11)
Dallas Mavericks (2011–14)
Memphis Grizzlies (2014–17)
Sacramento Kings (2017–18)
Atlanta Hawks (2018–20)

(Sources: stats-espn.com; Wikipedia)

The Making of Vince Carter

Vince Carter's Awards and Honors

1994–95 Mainland High School Band Drum Major
1994 Volleyball Conference Player-of-the-Year
1994–95 Florida's Mr. Basketball
1995 McDonald's All-America
1995 Parade All-America
1995 USA Today All-America
1995 Finalist, James Naismith High School Player-of-the-Year
1995 Gatorade Player-of-the-Year
1995 USA Junior National Select Basketball Team
1995 McDonald's All-America Slam Dunk Champion
1997 and 1998 Played in two NCAA Final Fours
1998 Ranked 18th nationally with a 59.1 field goal percentage
1998 First team, All Atlantic Coast Conference (ACC)
1998 Second team, All-America
1998 Candidate for the John R. Wooden Award
1998 Drafted #5 in the NBA
1999 NBA Rookie-of-the-Year
1999 *Sporting News* Rookie-of-the-Year

2000 NBA Slam Dunk Champion
2000 Child-Advocate-of-the-Year (Children's' Home Society)
2000 Olympic Gold Medalist (USA)
2000—3rd Team All-NBA
2001—2nd Team All-NBA
2000–08 Tied NBA All-Star Selection
2000 University of North Carolina Jersey #15 honored in the Dean Dome Rafters
2004 *Sporting News* Good Guys
2004 Named Goodwill Ambassador by Big Brothers/Big Sisters of America
2007 Florida High School Athletic Association Hall of Fame
2007 Florida Governor's Points of Light Award
2016 Twyman-Stokes Teammate-of-the-Year
2019–20 NBA Sportsmanship Award
2019 Daytona Beach Chamber Glenn Ritchey Award
2020 NBA Sportsmanship Award
2021 *USA Today*, 75 Greatest NBA Players
8-time NBA All-Star

About the Author

I doubt that anyone thinks about the end of their life on the day that they are born. Nor does a person ponder what will be the highlights or low-lights along the way.

I was born at Mount Sinai Hospital in Miami Beach, to Peggy and William "Willie" Harris, and grew up in Miami, Florida. I am the eldest of three daughters. My parents were hardworking people. My father's three girls were the apple of his eye. My mother ruled with a heavy hand, was a stickler for education and dressed neatly and appropriately whenever we stepped out of our home. Now that I look back on my life, it feels as if our childhood friends looked up to my family, even after my parents divorced and my mother remarried my wonderful stepfather, Clinton Green.

My sisters and I all went to college and were very active in high school activities, including intramural sports. Being involved in school and church activities was our ticket to get out and socialize. It was Peggy's rule that if you were breathing and could walk, you were going to be in school and church.

In 1972, my parents brought me to Daytona Beach, Florida, to attend Bethune-Cookman College. I completed my studies in 3.5 years and attained a Bachelor of Science degree in Business Education.

After college, instead of teaching, I took employment as an Administrative Assistant in the Personnel Department at Brunswick Corporation in DeLand, Florida. In the late 1970s, Brunswick Corporation was a defense plant that made camouflage nets. The company garnered federal contracts, as well as contracts from U.S. allies throughout the world. After a year, I was promoted to be the Engineering Department's Administrative Assistant and was privy to the detailed specs on how the camouflage nets were made. This information was classified, so a security clearance was necessary. This was quite a learning curve for me, fresh out of college, but I nailed it.

In 1976 I decided that it was time to start my teaching career as a business educator and had a few assignments helping students get on the right track, which entailed school-wide discipline. I enjoyed 21 years of educating students.

After Vince Carter became the fifth pick in the National Basketball Association's draft in 1998, it took approximately five months to agree the terms on the collective bargaining agreement. During that time, it was one of my tasks to help Vince establish and register his Embassy of Hope Foundation. I became the executive director of this organization, and I remain in this position to date.

In addition, I hold the position of chief executive officer of Visions in Flight (VIF), Inc., which is another Vince Carter company. My role with VIF is to oversee many of Vince Carter's business endeavors, including his major personal contributions. Some of the more notable are the Vince Carter Athletic Center on the campus of his high school alma mater, Mainland High School and the Vince Carter Sanctuary, which is the home of Project Warm—a residential behavioral substance abuse rehabilitation center for women. This facility includes the Michelle Carter-Scott Multipurpose Building. Vince Carter's Lettermen's Lane is located next to the Dean E. Smith Center on the campus of the University of North Carolina. Vince Carter's Restaurant, for 6 years, was one of the finest restaurants in the Daytona Beach, FL, area. It was my job to purchase the property, oversee the architectural design of the building, layout and interior design; and supervise the day-to-day operations of the restaurant.

The Making of Vince Carter

Sources

Atlanta Hawks
ESPN.com
National Federation of State High School Associations
National Collegiate Athletic Association (NCAA)
Sports-reference.com
USA Basketball

The Making of Vince Carter